THE MEASURE OF LIBRARY EXCELLENCE

*Linking the Malcolm Baldrige
Criteria and Balanced Scorecard
Methods to Assess Service Quality*

Despina Dapias Wilson,
Theresa del Tufo *and*
Anne E.C. Norman

McFarland & Company, Inc., Publishers
Jefferson, North Carolina, and London

LIBRARY OF CONGRESS CATALOGUING-IN-PUBLICATION DATA

Wilson, Despina Dapias, 1965–
The measure of library excellence : linking the
Malcolm Baldrige Criteria and Balanced Scorecard methods
to assess service quality / Despina Dapias Wilson,
Theresa del Tufo and Anne E.C. Norman.
p.   cm.
Includes bibliographical references and index.

ISBN-13: 978-0-7864-3036-9
softcover : 50# alkaline paper ∞

1. Libraries — Evaluation.   2. Public services (Libraries) — Evaluation.
3. Library planning.   4. Organizational effectiveness — Evaluation.
5. Organizational change — Management.   I. Del Tufo, Theresa, 1943–
II. Norman, Anne E.C., 1956–   III. Title

Z678.85.W55   2008   025.1 — dc22   2007030962

British Library cataloguing data are available

Cover photograph ©2006 Comstock Images

Manufactured in the United States of America

*McFarland & Company, Inc., Publishers
Box 611, Jefferson, North Carolina 28640
www.mcfarlandpub.com*

The Measure
of Library Excellence

This book is dedicated to the Honorable Ruth Ann Minner, governor of the state of Delaware, for providing guidance and leadership to the Delaware Quality Award program, and to Dr. Harriet Smith Windsor, Delaware's secretary of state, for her support of the Division of Libraries' quality project. This book is written in honor of the former Delaware secretary of labor and our friend, the Honorable Harold E. Stafford, for his unwavering support of performance excellence for state government and his genuine concern and affection for all the people who had the good fortune of working under his leadership.

Finally, we dedicate this book to our families, for their love, patience and unconditional support. Their generous spirit and profound belief in us empowered us to pursue our dreams.

Acknowledgments

It takes a considerable amount of work, creativity, research, and collaboration with experts to produce a work of this magnitude. Although the authors had the initial concept of presenting these two powerful approaches to performance excellence together, they had to build on the ideas and innovations of other writers and scholars in the field.

We are grateful to the following experts and organizations for sharing their knowledge and expertise, and for partnering with us to produce a document that will advance the state of knowledge for libraries and the communities they serve.

- V. Daniel Hunt, author of *Quality Management for Government: A Guide to Federal, State, and Local Implementation* (1992), for allowing us to modify the steps in developing and implementing quality so that we could apply them to public libraries.

- Dr. David Sirota, Brian Usilaner, and Michelle S. Weber, authors of the *Harvard Business Review* article "Sustaining Quality Improvement" (1994) for giving us their permission to include their concept of the elements of a quality culture as part of our text.

- Ralph Smith, vice president of Strategic Services for Orion Development Group, for giving us permission to adopt his Balanced Scorecard implementation method (C.A.R.D.), which he employed in teaching this dynamic approach.

- Delaware Division of Revenue, Department of Finance, State of Delaware, for allowing us to use some of their organizational results in the Business Results category of the Baldrige Template. A special thanks to Bill MacLachlan for inspiring us to experiment with the Baldrige system and for his generous spirit and willingness to share his vast knowledge and expertise.

- Debbie Neff, a consummate editor, for her skill, patience, tenacity, and sense of humor that made the task of editing the book an enjoyable journey rather than a stressful and tedious task.

Acknowledgments

- To Dr. Mark L. Blazey, for giving us permission to use his graphic representation of the Baldrige Criteria and for providing us with the initial training on the subject.
- To Paul Arveson and the Balanced Scorecard Institute, for allowing us to include key information and concepts on the Balanced Scorecard, which were brilliantly discussed in his 1999 article "Translating Performance Metrics from the Private to the Public Sector."

Contents

Contents

Preface

"Common sense is not so common."
— Voltaire (1694–1778)

In this book we will share with you the lessons we learned in applying the quality approach to our organization. We will explain the "what" and the "how" and provide information about our experience from a library's point of view to make this book relevant to those in the library community, but the methodologies outlined here apply to any size and type of organization.

What seems to be common sense to us right now was not so common when we first started on our quality journey. Our philosophical "common sense" conclusion was that there is no *one way* of doing business, but rather a combination of systems and tools that must be applied — in sequence — for an organization to have any kind of sustainability, continuous improvement, and performance excellence.

Our quality journey was certainly not smooth sailing all the time. We experienced many emotions, from frustration due to confusion, chaos, and resistance to inquiry, experimentation and discovery, to joy and enthusiasm for learning, empowerment and commitment. After taking the complex and expensive way ourselves, we want to show readers the simple and not so expensive way of doing exactly what we did, but in a shorter period of time.

Ponder the simplicity of this: In order to go from good to great, we must first identify what can catapult us to greatness (i.e., Baldrige Criteria). Second, we must have a system that can facilitate how we organize, prioritize, and record our findings to monitor how we are progressing toward our goals (i.e., Balanced Scorecard). Third, we need to monitor our progress by using measurement and process management tools that will enable us to actually assess and determine where we stand in reference to our strategic objectives (i.e., Six Sigma, LEAN, and flowcharting, to name just a few).

In taking the quality approach it is important to differentiate between a tool

1

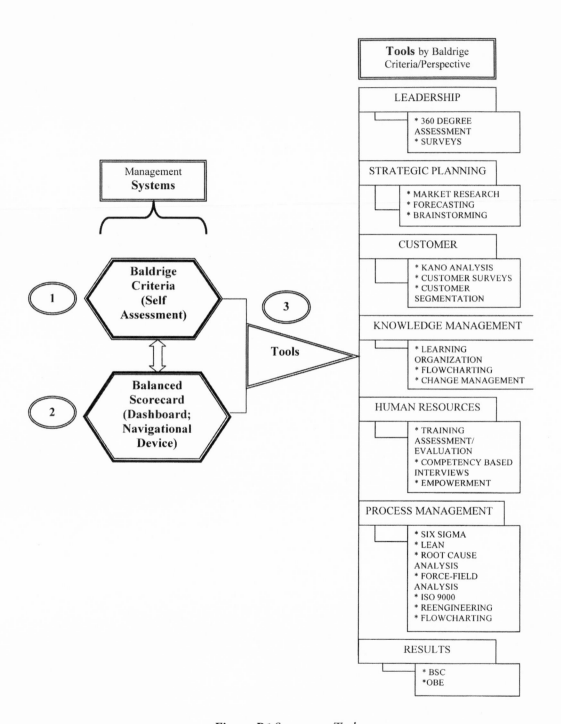

Figure P.1 *Systems vs. Tools.*

and a system. Simply stated, the Baldrige Criteria and the Balanced Scorecard are organizational management *systems*, whereas Six Sigma, Lean, flowcharting, and brainstorming are the *tools* that help us measure the progress toward our target. This concept is illustrated by Figure P.1.—Systems v. Tools.

Our goal in this book is to walk readers through these two systems, one step at a time, and to explain their implementation in simple, easy to understand words. This is why we have dedicated the seven chapters by Theresa del Tufo in Part I to the Baldrige Criteria and the five chapters by Despina Wilson in Part II to the Balanced Scorecard, with introductions to each part by Anne E.C. Norman.

Despina Dapias Wilson
Theresa del Tufo
Anne E.C. Norman
Fall 2007

Introduction

Many organizations have attempted to adopt quality models, only to fail in the end. Many times, they rested on their past triumphs and became apathetic and mediocre. They neglected to consider the changing internal and external environments and failed to improve and sustain their past performance. Oftentimes, in their despair to fix monumental problems, they experimented and jumped from one performance improvement approach to another, only to experience short-lived success and exacerbate an already chaotic situation.

Libraries are no different. We must all agree that no matter what industry we talk about, whether an organization is for-profit, non-profit or public, the collection of data and their effective use can significantly improve the organization's planning, decision making, management, and performance.

This book brings to light a whole new approach to performance assessment and improvement by combining two proven and time-tested theories: the Malcolm Baldrige Criteria and the Balanced Scorecard. The application of this powerful combination is what makes this book unique, dynamic, and potentially useful. Furthermore, the two theories are broken down and explained step-by-step for easy understanding. It doesn't just stop at assessing an organization; it provides a system through which all the findings and performance measures can be organized in a logical, cause-and-effect sequence. Other sources may describe just the Baldrige Criteria or just the Balanced Scorecard and stop, leaving the organization with many questions and no real guidance as to where to start.

Although the Balanced Scorecard was originally developed for private business, it is increasingly being used by public and non-profit organizations, including libraries. In 2001 the Association of Research Libraries (ARL) and the Online Computer Library Services (OCLC) conducted a three-day workshop with a primary focus on the Balanced Scorecard. Also, according to the German Research Association, several German libraries are using it as well. Currently, the National Center for Education Statistics (NCES) and the National Center for Library and Information Science (NCLIS) are studying and are interested in the Balanced Scorecard and the potential benefits it may bring. The state of California, through a grant from the Institute of Museum and Library Services, hired a consultant who wrote a manual on how to develop a Balanced Scorecard for libraries.

The University of Virginia Library (UVL) implemented the Balanced Scorecard in 2001 as a support mechanism for developing a culture of assessment. By adopting the BSC, the library was forced to focus on measures that really made a difference in improving its strategic performance. Just like any other library, it had an overabundance of collected data that were not being used to manage performance and support fact-based decision-making. The majority of the data involved information about the users or the customers. The UVL realized that its data collection was "unbalanced," and that it had not paid attention to other areas like the development of its staff, its processes, and its financial health.

Although UVL is still using the Balanced Scorecard, the adaptation rate of a culture of assessment across the board has been slow. James Self, director of Management Information Services at the university, noted in an article written in 2004 that "it would be premature to claim that we have achieved a culture of assessment." Note that this article was written three years *after* the library first implemented the scorecard.

We strongly believe that one of the reasons UVL's adaptation rate is slow may be due to the fact that it probably did not do a Baldrige-like self-assessment before it decided to implement the Balanced Scorecard. We predict that the state of California may experience a similar internal resistance. Eventually, the assessment culture in these organizations will come about, but at a much slower rate than for those organizations that adopted the Baldrige Criteria, first.

This is where our experience and approach could prove valuable. If a manager first understands the components that make up a quality organization and knows how his or her organization measures up to the Baldrige Criteria, then he or she will have an easier time adopting a monitoring and performance system like the Balanced Scorecard.

In recent years, numerous Delaware state agencies have won a Baldrige First State Quality award, including the Department of Labor, the Division of Health and Social Services and the State Personnel Training division, but currently the Delaware State Library is the only winning agency using the Balanced Scorecard. The winner of the top award, the "Bill Gore Award" (named after Bill Gore, the inventor of Gortex material) which is the highest in-state Baldrige award, was the Division of Revenue, a division of the Department of Finance. All award recipients reported tremendous results by applying the Baldrige Criteria to their key operational processes, but are still lacking a comprehensive measurement methodology to organize and report their data in a systematic way. This is why the other winners are starting to get interested and are keeping a close eye on the progress of the Delaware State Library's automated Balanced Scorecard system.

The adoption of the Baldrige Criteria before the implementation of the Balanced Scorecard differentiates our approach from that of other entities that are experiencing a slower rate of progress. Although libraries and other agencies have adopted various methods of outcome measurements, they totally miss the point by neglecting to assess the quality of the organization first. The quality approach looks at the organization as an interactive and cohesive system, where improvements in one part affect all the other interdependent parts. Before implementing the Balanced Scorecard, it is important to make sure that the organization has a solid infrastructure to support this system-wide assessment. Is there a committed and visionary leadership who engages in strategic planning and develops realistic strategic goals? Are the processes efficient and effective and are there well-trained and competent employees to do the work? Do leaders, employees, and processes support a customer-focused culture that values customer preferences, requirements and satisfaction?

Just like a doctor must diagnose the patient's condition (i.e., get to know his or her health history and symptoms of the disease) before prescribing medication, organizations must self-assess their baseline condition before knowing which performance and strategic measures to use to monitor their progress in achieving their goals. Although targeted measures can be identified by using only the Baldrige Criteria, they may not be "balanced" or comprehensive enough to measure all critical areas that need to be accounted for to get a good picture of the organization's total effectiveness profile. Also, the measures may not be aligned with the organization's mission, vision, objectives, initiatives, and even budget, without a complementary methodology such as the Balanced Scorecard.

While reading this book, we urge you to leave behind all your pre-conceived ideas about quality, numbers, and performance measurements, and try to soak up the simplicity and logic of the Baldrige Criteria for performance excellence and the preciseness and power of the Balanced Scorecard measurement system. "Follow the Yellow Brick Road" (see conclusion).

What follows next is a series of frequently asked questions. Usually these are found at the end of a book, but we took a different route, only to help readers obtain — from the beginning — a little more clarity as to what unfolds in the coming chapters.

Frequently Asked Questions

How does the Balanced Scorecard compare to the Baldrige Criteria?

The Baldrige organizational readiness assessment must be done prior to the development of the Balanced Scorecard. The data gathered by the assessment reveal the organization's Strengths, Weaknesses, Opportunities and Threats (SWOT), and therefore provide a foundation for the strategic measures that need to be monitored for mission success. Furthermore, the Balanced Scorecard is an excellent framework to help with the alignment of the strategy, mission, vision, measures, targets, budget, and initiatives, which in turn will be sorted into four perspectives — Customer, Internal Processes, Knowledge and Growth, and Financial.

How does the Balanced Scorecard compare with Six Sigma?

As noted above, the Balanced Scorecard is a framework which facilitates the alignment of strategy, mission, vision, measures, targets, budget, and initiatives. The Six Sigma management approach is a set of tools that provide various techniques and methods for measuring results. As part of the "sequence of learning," the steps we recommend are: 1) Baldrige assessment first; 2) Balanced Scorecard second; and 3) Six Sigma, OBE and other tools third. Six Sigma ought to be the final step because an organization would not know what the strategic measures are without going through steps one and two first. See figure P.1, which illustrates the sequence and differences between "systems" and "tools."

We use the Outcome Based Evaluation (OBE) method, so do we need Baldrige Criteria and the Balanced Scorecard as well?

Yes. While OBE is an excellent tool to develop the outcome-oriented results of a program, it only represents a fraction of the whole operating picture. It does not address the enablers that will make OBE successful (such as the effectiveness and efficiency of the internal processes, level of adequate funding, or the condition — levels of training and empowerment — of the human resource piece). In the simplest of terms, such enablers are an operationally sound organization and alignment of programming and strategy. There could very well be a program that has been developed to fit the outcome-based structure perfectly, but might be totally unaligned with and unrelated to the library's overall mission and strategy. The Baldrige Criteria and the Balanced Scorecard are the soil with the right acidity balance in which to plant the OBE seed.

Is there proof that the Baldrige Criteria works in libraries?

Yes. The Delaware Division of Libraries applied the Baldrige Criteria (along with the Balanced Scorecard) and won the Quality Commitment Award for Excellence in 2004. The division applied the Baldrige Criteria again in 2005 but this time it incorporated all lessons learned, paying close attention to the recommended improvements suggested in the 2004 Delaware Quality Award Examiner Feedback Report. This time the division won the Merit Award, which indicates that the organization is well on its way to becoming a quality organization and that some of the processes can serve as models of operation.

Is the Baldrige assessment something a library branch manager could do, or something that a system director would have to put in place?

Organizations that have applied the Baldrige Criteria use different approaches in their self-assessment and implementation processes. Some engage all staff in the process, some select participants from a cross section of functions and levels, and some appoint a small group to represent all of their colleagues.

Why would libraries invest the time?

It is time to change the way libraries analyze, align, and present their data. Furthermore, the performance excellence solution is the most straightforward method for producing results and strategically monitoring progress. If things are managed and done the way they have always been, nothing is going to change, and libraries will eventually be swallowed up by competition (like Google, Amazon.com, Borders, etc.). Change will only happen if the management system changes. The same old ways will yield the same old results and outcomes. Currently libraries utilize a potpourri of data, measures, styles, and systems, but if methods were to be aligned, the value of library services would become visible and, most important, "provable."

What are the benefits of the Balanced Scorecard approach?

- Better utilization of resources: It improves the efficiency and effectiveness of processes and therefore reduces the cycle time of completing tasks and offering services, and also saves money.
- Alignment of strategic objectives and activities with the strategic plan: It is a communication tool that provides real-time decision-making information.
- Prioritization: By using the Baldrige assessment process, managers can systematically identify operational gaps and critical priorities for improvements.
- Organizational assessment: It allows managers to identify areas of good and mediocre performance, allowing greater focus on areas that need to be improved the most.

- Increased control and reduced risk: It reduces decision-making risk by providing accurate and real-time information when it is needed.
- Transparency of information and visibility to all levels of the organization: Staff are held accountable, which fuels the motivation for employees to do better and be innovative. Guidance and decision-making are based on solid data and not hearsay and rumors.
- Identification of organizational strengths: It promotes the organization's competitive edge by comparing itself to the best of similar organizations. By benchmarking, organizations can promote the use of best practices to drive up performance. There's nothing like healthy competition!
- Higher Baldrige score: The Baldrige scoring system allots 450 out of the 1,000 points to the results section. An organization may be addressing all six of the Baldrige Criteria successfully, but without a systematic and aligned measurement system producing results, the final score can be very low.

Are there any disadvantages to the Balanced Scorecard?

Yes, just as there are challenges associated with any organizational change. It is more difficult and challenging to implement a Balanced Scorecard in a larger, more diversified organization than a smaller one, simply because the larger ones are more complex. Whatever the case may be, the change will first require the commitment of the top leaders, eventually the commitment of all staff, and finally the availability of funding. However, once it is in place, the Balanced Scorecard becomes much easier to maintain, especially when it is automated.

What are some pitfalls to the Balanced Scorecard?

It cannot be understood and applied correctly if the organization has not been trained on the quality principles and gone through the Baldrige Criteria assessment and application process first. As a consequence of not being understood:

- It can become too measure-focused instead of strategy-focused.
- Garbage in, garbage out: Current or meaningless measures may be evaluated and assessed instead of those measures which support the organization's strategy, mission and vision. As a result, the Balanced Scorecard will most likely not be a useful tool for everyday decision-making and will end up as "shelf-ware."
- Staff scorecards can be used by leaders to micromanage, which could stifle innovation and empowerment.

- If not automated, the Balanced Scorecard has greater chances of eventually failing due to the time and effort needed to manually gather and post data from the various data sources and maintain all cascaded scorecards.

Isn't the Balanced Scorecard a fad?

The Balanced Scorecard was developed in the early 1990s and is still being implemented and adopted by many organizations today. It has stood the test of time because it is based on fundamental principles of management to have a strategy in place, then measure, monitor, and analyze results, and use the feedback for continuous improvement. The methods may change, but the concept will be around forever.

I am a librarian. What's in it for me?

A librarian is no different than any other program manager. At any one point in time, a program manager may be handling multiple programs. This is where the Balanced Scorecard can help. It not only helps to track whether a program is on time and within budget, but it also shows the clear linkage between the overall performance and how it contributes to the overall strategic plan. Besides, by monitoring the program through the Balanced Scorecard, in the end managers will have good, hard facts to defend their programs and show their progress toward the desired outcomes. In addition, the strategy map can be used as a guide to manage and monitor results and to maximize outcomes. The Balanced Scorecard also gives you control — if you are the expert in your program area, you own it, and you are the best person to define the kind of measures used to monitor success.

Is the Balanced Scorecard relevant to government agencies?

Absolutely. In today's information society, citizens are not only demanding accountability and quality service as to how public funding is used, but they also expect to be able to get information about government performance promptly. They also expect a greater return on investment for tax dollars spent. Since Congress passed a series of crosscutting management laws in the 1990s, such as the Government Performance Results Act of 1993, government agencies have had to re-invent themselves and think more like private industry. Many government organizations adopted various qualitative methods in hopes of fixing and continuously improving their organizational performance, but with no results. In many instances, they ignored systemic issues that may have been the real culprits of failure. Failure could have been avoided had they taken the time to assess the organization's performance and methods of operation by using the Baldrige assessment exercise.

How long does it take to implement the Balanced Scorecard system?

With the guidance of expert Baldrige and Balance Scorecard facilitators it is estimated that implementation can take anywhere from four months to more than two years, depending on the condition or results of a "gap analysis" of the organization. In general, it takes about three weeks for the management review, the assessment of the organization, and the determination on how resources will be committed. During the fourth week, implementation teams should have been selected; during the fifth through the seventh weeks, team orientation and training should take place; during the eighth through thirty-second weeks, new processes should be created and the Balanced Scorecard developed and implemented. Kaplan and Norton estimate it will take 26 months for full deployment of the Balanced Scorecard from the top leadership down to the level of individual employees.

Is there a list of measures that I can select for our Balanced Scorecard?

No. The Balanced Scorecard is not pre-canned. The measures are strictly defined by an organization's mission, vision, and the process by which a manager develops the strategic plan. In other words, what is important to one organization may not be important to another, even if the organizations have the same mission. This can be due to particular challenges the organization is facing at the time. The framework of the scorecard is the same, but the contents may differ.

What are the budgetary implications of implementing a Balanced Scorecard?

Because the Balanced Scorecard helps align all of the organization's resources and activities, it actually helps with the strategic allocation of funds, and in turn yields a greater return on investment. The Balanced Scorecard framework allows the organization to be flexible. Due to its dynamic ability to continuously monitor the performance of each measure, the Balanced Scorecard can help with shifting and re-allocating funds when and where they are needed the most without the manager having to go through an in-depth budget review process every time a change is necessary.

How can we ensure the sustainability of our Balanced Scorecard?

The Baldrige and Balanced Scorecard processes are intended to be used on an ongoing basis and involve a continuous improvement cycle that never ends. The feedback from the Baldrige assessment provides the fuel for the Balanced Scorecard. Note that it is important to keep up with the training and re-education of leadership and staff about the purposes and benefits of implementing such a system. As long as the focus is maintained on the organization's mission, vision, and strategy (which do not change often), the "system" will be consistent, and the organization will only get better with time. The real question is, once the organization knows the right things to do, will the current leadership have the discipline to do the right thing? Conversely, but equally important, will the current leadership stop doing the wrong things? If so, the assessment culture will become second nature and the Balanced Scorecard will be routinely used for everyday decision-making. It is also important to point out that at some point in time (better sooner than later), the Balanced Scorecard must be automated because it can become very time consuming and cumbersome to collect, align, and monitor objectives and measures from multiple cascading scorecards.

Part I

The Baldrige Criteria
for Performance Excellence

1

Introduction to the Baldrige Criteria

"If you have knowledge, let others light their candles at it."
— Margaret Fuller

"Where are our libraries ranked now? *Sixtieth* in the nation?"

The question rang out from an official during our 2002 State Budget Hearing. Despite the best efforts of the Delaware Division of Libraries and with significant support from the state administration and legislature, Delaware public libraries still come in near the bottom of the National Center for Education Statistics (NCES) national rankings. NCES is the federal agency that coordinates national library data collection and ranking. Delaware is ranked high — eighth — in the nation for state operating income per capita, yet low in numerous other area (e.g., 2003 per capita, forty-third in book and serial volumes; forty-seventh in reference transactions; fifty-first in staffing).

State library agencies throughout the nation are responsible for library development and for helping libraries to improve performance. It was time to get to the bottom of Delaware's problems — to uncover what was causing our poor performance in the rankings and to help our libraries to truly achieve excellence. Our quality-learning journey began....

The staff of the Delaware Division of Libraries joined the Delaware Quality Partnership, a grassroots organization of state and the private sector employees interested in learning about best practices that businesses use to achieve excellence. Through grants from the First State Quality Improvement Fund, we hired consultants to assist us in learning about quality systems, listening to the voice of the customer, and learning about process improvements and other quality tools. The

This introduction was written by Anne E.C. Norman.

Delaware Division of Libraries invited the library community — staff, friends, and trustees — to accompany us on our quality-learning journey.

The Baldrige Criteria for Performance Excellence, which "quality" is based on, consists of hundreds of "how" questions. *How* do we update our strategic plan? *How* do we ensure customers are satisfied? *How* do we ensure employees are satisfied? The list seemed endless. The criteria consist of questions, not answers. Learning how to develop processes to answer the questions was aided by training, but was also very much dependent upon our own resourcefulness.

Fortunately, we're librarians! We have the books and information at our disposal in our libraries to help us learn how to address the criteria so that we can improve our organization to achieve results. We are learning to be a learning organization and to tap into the resources in our libraries for our own benefit. Throughout our quality-learning journey, we have relied upon several books that we will be recommending in hopes that they will be helpful to you. Unfortunately, our learning did not follow a linear path.

To help readers avoid our pitfalls, we have sequenced the events of our story in the order in which we wish they had occurred. Should you decide to embark on your own quality-learning journey, following our suggested path will save you both time and frustration.

For the Customer

In 2002, our agency started a program entitled "If All the Delaware Library Community Read the Same Book" to start orienting our staff and other stakeholders to the quality approach. A title is selected annually as a professional development tool and to communicate to the library community the challenges and opportunities that the Delaware Division of Libraries staff perceive might occur in the near future. *Be Our Guest: Perfecting the Art of Customer Service* — or BOG as we affectionately called it — by the Disney Institute was the first book we assigned in our program.

Using BOG as a tool, we held numerous workshops for the library community throughout the year so we could learn how the "backstage" processes and systems affect our customers' experiences. Which systems are we concerned about? Do we focus our efforts on library catalogs, Inter Library Loan (ILL), reference, or programming? Many of our systems have been around for so long that they had become invisible and were taken for granted.

Innovation

Diffusion of Innovations (1962) by Everett Rogers reassured us that we didn't have to have everyone on board at the start. Joining us on our quality-learning journey were the "Innovators" and "Early Adopters." We had to go back to pick up the others, the "Early Majority," "Late Majority," and "Laggards," once we had applied our learning and had developed new processes.

I attended training sponsored by the State of Delaware, Duke Executive Leadership for State Executives, and learned about "Symbols" and "Stretch Targets." In small group work, my colleagues from throughout state government suggested to me that a library card could be our visual symbol and stretch target for everyone to rally around. When they asked me how many Delawareans have a library card, I couldn't answer them; we had never collected that information. When we went back to the office and queried libraries to find out, we learned that less than *half* of Delawareans had a library card at that time, so that became our baseline figure. We selected an agency vision to guide our future, which states, "Every Delawarean will have a library card, and will use it often!" As I shared this vision with the library community for their feedback, we uncovered capacity problems that we needed to address. I was greeted by some librarians with the cautious remark, "Not more *people*! We can't handle any more people!" If we wanted Delaware libraries to be first in the nation, we had to define what that really meant.

As state librarian, I have the responsibility for good libraries although I do not have the governing and decision making authority to make good libraries happen. As in most states, libraries in Delaware report to a menagerie of governing authorities — city, county and numerous independent libraries. I'm in charge of "herding cats" — in Delaware it's known as "herding chickens" or encouraging all of the libraries to work together and to move forward in the same direction. I approached my job like a CEO and extrapolated best practices from various business models. What could we learn about franchise organizations, for instance, that would help us strengthen our library processes?

We contracted with Himmel & Wilson and with Providence Associates to develop a statewide master plan for library services and construction. We wanted to obtain all of the information about the libraries at one time and use the aggregated data in our decision making. This project entailed building a statewide, integrated framework for library services and construction, assimilating state and local governance, creating a common language, and defining terms, including tiers of libraries, library services, funding, staffing, operating costs, maintenance, measures, performance indicators, renovations, remodeling, combined facilities, patron policies, and collections. The overall goal was to develop a plan that incorporated best practices for library services and construction, manage costs, equalize ongoing library development, and provide seamless integrated and equal access to library resources for all Delawareans. Whew!

Developing our master plan involved the most extensive study of its kind ever conducted in the nation. That's the benefit of being in a small state. We have more information than we've ever had at one time about the libraries, including profiles of each library. The master plan is like holding a mirror up to all the libraries, so that they can determine if they like what they see individually, collectively, and in comparison to others.

Statewide Master Plan
for Library Services and Construction, 2005
Key Findings and Recommendations

Telephone survey conducted by the University of Delaware revealed:

- 92 percent of library users and 84 percent of non-library users said libraries are "vital" or "very important" to the quality of life in their community
- "Delaware's library collections are too small and are out of date"
- "Almost without exception, Delaware's public libraries are badly under-staffed"
  Total paid FTEs per 25,000 population.
  2001 — 50th
  2002 — 50th
  2003 — 51st
- "Delaware has too many library buildings but less than half of the library space needed to offer high quality library service." [Goal is one square foot per capita].
- "Twenty-two libraries are less than 10,000 square feet, of which 13 libraries are 5,000 SF or less." [Goal is a minimum of 10,000 square feet per library]
- "Unless a concerted effort is made to improve library services quickly, Delaware is likely to fall further behind because of its significant population growth"

Recommendation — Establish anchor libraries, at a minimum of one in each county to serve a support role with in-depth collections and reference materials.

We involved all of our stakeholders in strategic planning for the LSTA five-year federal plan for 2003 through 2007, including the public libraries, the Council on Libraries, local advisory boards, and the Friends of the Library. We aligned

all of the plans — LSTA, state, technology, and the new state library master plan —
to ensure that they worked together and were all-encompassing.

The Library's Core Purpose — Collections to Inform, Educate, and Entertain

Two publications that we examined and discussed to help ensure that we were
operating around the libraries central purpose were *Competing for the Future* by
Gary Hamel and C.K. Prahalad (1994) and *Get Back in the Box: Innovation from
the Inside Out* by Douglas Rushkoff (2005).

What business are we in? Typically librarians are very philosophical about our
purpose in society. We provide access to information for all regardless of economic
circumstance; we protect the public's right to know in a democracy; and we support literacy so that all may possess the ability to read. Through our quality journey, we've learned that we must identify our core business and core competencies
in concrete terms in order to measure our impact and affect improvements. We facilitated a discussion with members of the library community in which we peeled back
the layers of emotion and pride over what we do in order to identify our core purpose. It wasn't easy, but after extensive debate we came to a consensus — that is, the
library's core purpose consists of collections, in all formats, to inform, educate, and
entertain patrons. We agreed to this definition for testing purposes so that we could
measure it and examine the key results we obtained.

All of the services that libraries provide support and are inextricably linked to
our core business purpose. Services and processes and every aspect of our enterprise are focused on, aligned with, and link back to the core mission. In our model,
the next layer surrounding the core of collections consists of reference and reader's
advisory. Reference librarians assist the public in finding information in our collections. Reader's advisory staff links readers with their ideal reads in our collections.

The next layer consists of programming. Libraries provide programs that entice
the public to explore our collections and that assist in applying information from
our collections. In Delaware, we developed a best practices for programming kit to
encourage libraries to display items that pertain to their programs and to encourage program participants to obtain a library card, if they don't already have one.
Proactively linking programming with the collection increases library card regis-
tration and circulation. Libraries should ensure that the topic is well represented
in their collections when designing a program.

The external layer consists of outreach and partnering. In Delaware our best practices for partnering include collaboratively developing a bibliography of items in Delaware libraries on the subjects of interest to our partners. We show our partners what materials already exist in Delaware libraries on the subjects of interest, and request their feedback on what ought to be added to the collections. For outreach, we experiment with live library card sign-up and check-out of material at partners' or partners-to-be events, conferences, and book fairs.

Using collection data from the Delaware Library Catalog, we plan to develop new programs based on subjects with high circulation. We also plan to conduct a programming needs assessment in our communities to determine additional subjects of interest. We'll use our findings to augment our collections and program offerings to entice new users to our libraries.

Operational Excellence

From *The Discipline of Market Leaders* (1995) by Michael Treacy and Frederick D. Wiersema we learned that organizations should select three areas to work on but really focus on one in particular to achieve excellence. Delaware libraries selected to focus on the following priority areas: customer intimacy, product leadership, and operational excellence. Customer intimacy entails developing an in-depth knowledge of customer preferences, requirements and level of satisfaction. Libraries are not likely to achieve excellence in this area since we don't retain information about our patrons' use, with the exception of patrons who are homebound or use the Library for the Blind and Physically Handicapped.

Product leadership requires a focus on innovation, such as innovations typical of companies like 3M, Google, and Amazon.com. Delaware libraries tend to depend on their vendors for innovation, and we didn't believe that we could achieve excellence in innovation at this time due to our limited staff and financial resources. The area we decided to focus on was operational excellence, which consists of distribution expertise such as that exhibited by Wal-Mart. Using the Delaware Library Catalog, we are focusing on collaborative collection development across libraries and user-friendliness. We are layering additional technologies, such as e-books, on a single unified system. We are also looking at staggering the hours that libraries are open to ensure reasonably convenient access within a geographical area. Achieving operational excellence will require a close look at all of our systems and processes, such as Inter Library Loan (ILL) delivery, book ordering, processing, and cataloging. Once we have updated all of our processes using the latest technologies, we'll then be able to direct our attention to building improved services upon a new, strong foundation.

Library Development

What is library development? We say that our mission at the Delaware Division of Libraries is library development, but we have had a difficult time defining it for our quality consultants. What does it really mean and what does it consist of? How do we know when we've achieved library development?

It would be helpful to have a model, similar to human development, of the distinct stages of library development. In Delaware we've cycled through the trends of state-based library standards and of local community planning. Ultimately, we'll end up with a model that includes both. The model should also encompass the basics as well as the evolution of libraries. Where do you start with new services, such as digitization, virtual reference, and electronic resources? We might capture the lessons learned and best practices in a more proactive and organized fashion so that libraries evolve much faster and keep up with developments occurring in today's world.

Where are we now in our developmental journey? I'm proud to say that due to the efforts of the staff, the Delaware Division of Libraries received the Delaware Quality Commitment Award in 2004 and the Delaware Quality Award of Merit in 2005. This signifies that we are on the right path and are making progress, although we still have a long way to go. This also signifies that the Baldrige Criteria can be applied in a public sector organization, such as a state library.

And the Delaware libraries quality learning journey continues...

Theresa Del Tufo wrote the next chapter of this book. She is one of the Delaware Division of Libraries' quality consultants, and we were able to hire her through a grant from the First State Quality Improvement Fund. Theresa facilitated and assisted the Delaware Division of Libraries in submitting its first application to the Delaware Quality Award assessment process.

Throughout 2004, we held "Tuesdays with Tes" where all Delaware Division of Libraries staff met in our training center and learned how to complete the sections of the application. During this period. the staff finally "got" what process improvement is all about. They stopped asking "What are we doing?" and began to report on process problems they experienced in other agencies, inn the marketplace, etc. Thanks to Theresa's devotion to our learning and our success, the Delaware Division of Libraries received the Delaware Quality Commitment Award for 2004.

2

Quality and the Baldrige Criteria: Why Adopt the Baldrige Way? What's in It for Libraries?

In times of change, learners inherit the earth, while the learned find themselves beautifully equipped to deal with a world that no longer exists."

— Eric Hoffer

Accountability to the Customer

A fundamental principle that high-performing organizations adopt to be successful is to provide quality services to its customers. For-profit organizations, governmental agencies and non-profit organizations are *all* accountable to their customers. Customers may be patrons, students, clients, voters, or consumers of goods, but in the end, they all demand accountability from the providers of services or products.

Studies conducted by the U.S. Office of Consumer Affairs reveal that 95 percent of dissatisfied customers walk away without ever complaining to the company but talk about their dissatisfaction to 12 of their friends. Worst of all, in today's Internet age a dissatisfied customer can tell thousands of people at once about his unpleasant experience. In *Customer Service*, customer expert Dr. Paul R. Timm contends, "No business or organization can succeed without building customer satisfaction and loyalty. Likewise, no person can make a good living without meeting the needs of customers" (p. 2). So, if the main ingredient of success is customer satisfaction, an organization must build a system where every input and output to the system contributes to that strategic target.

Chapters 2 through 8 were written by Theresa del Tufo.

Organizational Strategy

The principles of quality contend that in order for an organization to increase customer satisfaction, to improve customer loyalty, and to continue to bring in new customers (Category 3 — Customer Focus), there must be a system-wide effort to develop a well thought-out organizational strategy (Category 2 — Strategic Plan). But who is going to carry out the strategy? Motivated and highly trained employees are the ones who implement the plan since they are the ones who work closest to the process and know what needs to be done (Category 5 — Human Resources). How will leaders share the strategic plan with all the key stakeholders, employees, and managers? Organizations manage their knowledge base through the use of technology and a system wide communication plan (Category 4 — Knowledge Management). How will the strategic plan be carried out? The Baldrige way involves the use of efficient and effective processes that result in cost savings to the company and quality services to customers (Category 6 — Processes). Finally, how will the organization know if it is effective and successful? The quality approach is to have performance measures in place to monitor outcomes and to continuously improve performance (Category 7 — Organizational Results). Most of all, who will be the "glue" that holds everything together, the one who will keep the vision alive, empower and motivate employees, and make informed decisions that are critical to success? The Baldrige way says that the leader (Category 1 — Leadership) is the major driver who provides direction, vision, and leadership.

The above describes the application of the Baldrige Criteria to an organization. It is clear that no matter what type of organization we are talking about, these principles are applicable and will remain predominant in an information society. In 1987, after years of intensive research and testing, the U.S. Department of Commerce identified the key elements essential to organizational excellence, which are the basis of the Baldrige Quality Award Criteria. These criteria have since been adopted by all types of organizations in 40 American states and 55 countries throughout the world.

Having said all this, it is critical to remember that simply creating the "system" may not be enough. Its components must be interdependent. If each component works in isolation, the system will eventually fail. A process, for example, cannot only be state of the art, but must also contribute value to the organization and to the customer; if it does not meet these goals, no matter how perfect it is in other ways, the process must be eliminated.

The Courage to Survive and to Grow

Libraries are no different than any other entity when it comes to organizational excellence. The old way of doing business no longer works. Libraries are data rich, but information poor. In today's world, libraries are desperately in need of re-inventing who they are and how they do business. They need to improve services and public image exponentially in order to compete successfully with the internet and private enterprise, such as Amazon.com and Barnes and Noble. The dynamic combination of these two tested approaches to organizational success (Baldrige Criteria and Balanced Scorecard) is the answer to public libraries critical need to compete with private enterprise and to improve performance.

Some recent studies (including one by John Carlo Bertot, Charles R. McClure and Paul T. Yeager in 2004) noted that walk-in visits and circulation statistics may be declining due to the fact that a majority of libraries do not collect or report usage figures for network services. Bertot, McClure and Yeager noted that libraries are in a transitional phase — that is, "they continue to provide traditional services while simultaneously increasing network services and resources." Traditional indicators of effectiveness, such as library visits and reference transaction counts, are used as traditional measures, which are on a decreasing trend and do not reflect the total picture of the growth in library services. The key question for leaders in the library community is now to define what business they are in and where they want to go. They need to define a new operating model and a compelling vision of their future.

A recent survey conducted by the Delaware Division of Libraries (2005) revealed (Figure 2.1) that patrons do not use libraries for several reasons: they have had "no recent need" (54.9 percent), they get information from the Internet or elsewhere (40.8 percent), they have other sources for reading materials (39 percent) and they are too busy (26.2 percent). Studies conducted by the Hampshire County Council (2005) showed similar findings as to the most common reasons patrons do not use libraries. Respondents indicated that they have no time, they can get the information they need from the Internet, and they prefer to purchase their own books.

Are there areas where libraries are performing better? Of course, there are areas where they excel and are showing promising trends. The findings of a study conducted in 2002 by the University of Illinois Library Research Center (LRC) for the American Library Association (ALA) revealed the following positive indicators:

- Library patrons use the library an average of 13 times a year
- Sixty-two percent of adult Americans say they have a library card. Adults with children are most likely to have a library card (73 percent)
- Ninety-one percent believe libraries are changing and dynamic places with a variety of activities for the whole family

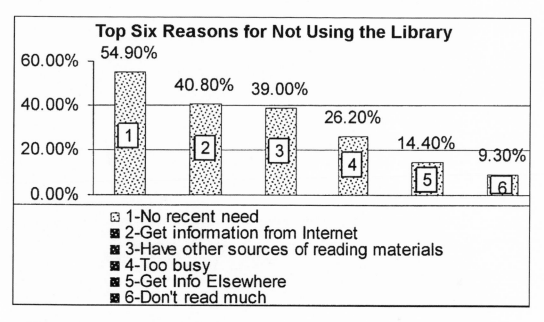

Figure 2.1 *Source: University of Illinois Library Research Center (LRC) for the American Library Association (2002).*

Figure 2.1 shows the responses of 1,000 adults who participated in the random-sample telephone survey conducted March 8–11, 2002.

3

What Is Quality? What Is Quality Management?

"The best is the enemy of the good."
—Voltaire (1694–1778)

As we discussed earlier, quality is a comprehensive and system-wide approach to assessing and improving an organization to enable it to provide and sustain quality services. We offer the following operational definition to guide readers as they pursue performance excellence and experience the quality journey: Quality is a comprehensive management approach that focuses on employee involvement, leadership, product and service excellence, continuous improvement, data-based decision making and process improvement, all designed to meet or exceed customer expectations.

V. Daniel Hunt, author of the book *Quality Management for Government* (1993), declared, "Quality management is not a minor refinement of past managerial practices. What sets quality management apart from other approaches to management is a genuine new perspective on how to best combine or reengineer the resources (people, budget, programs and processes) that make up a government organization" (p. 21). Quality management, Hunt noted, involves a "unique set of principles" and new roles for leaders and employees who are armed with new knowledge on how to continuously improve processes and outcomes (p. 21). At the center of this powerful new management principle is the focus on customers, who are the ultimate arbiters when it comes to quality. Customers define quality for the organization, employees design quality processes, and leadership provides the vision, direction and planning.

Quality management can only succeed when an organization decides to change its culture and values. It requires a paradigm shift from the traditional management leadership style and organizational structure. Organizations now have empowered and educated employees who have the responsibility and accountability to design and improve processes, and who work closest to the processes that need to be improved. Now that we're on the same page, let's look at the hard stuff.

The Baldrige National Quality Award Criteria

The quality approach, as defined by the Malcolm Baldrige National Quality Award Criteria, is the overarching framework that guides the organization as it pursues excellence in the areas of leadership, strategic planning, customer focus, knowledge management, human resources, key business processes, and organizational results.

The seven Baldrige Criteria and the critical linkages among them are portrayed in Figure 3.1. Leadership (Category 1), Strategic Planning (Category 2), and Customer and Market Focus (Category 3) emphasize the importance of a leadership focus on strategy and customers. Performance effectiveness starts with the driver triad of effective and committed leadership, realistic strategic plans, and satisfied customers.

Measurement, Analysis and Knowledge Management (Category 4) is the "brain center" of the high-performing organization and is critical to the effective management of an organization and its key business processes. Information is essential to monitoring performance against measurable goals set during the strategic planning process. Leaders use data to set priorities, allocate resources, and enhance decision making at all levels of the organization.

Employees, guided by effective and efficient key processes, accomplish the work of the organization that yields breakthrough performance results. Human Resource Focus (Category 5) and Process Management (Category 6) comprise the people and processes that produce Organizational Performance Results (Category 7).

All actions lead to Organizational Performance Results. Leaders must pay close attention to and learn from their organizational results in order to focus on the key priorities that drive continuous improvements.

The short description of the seven Baldrige Criteria will provide an overview of what's to come.

Category 1: Leadership (90 points)

The leadership category addresses ways in which senior leaders create and sustain a customer-focused quality culture that values empowerment, innovation, learning and public responsibility.

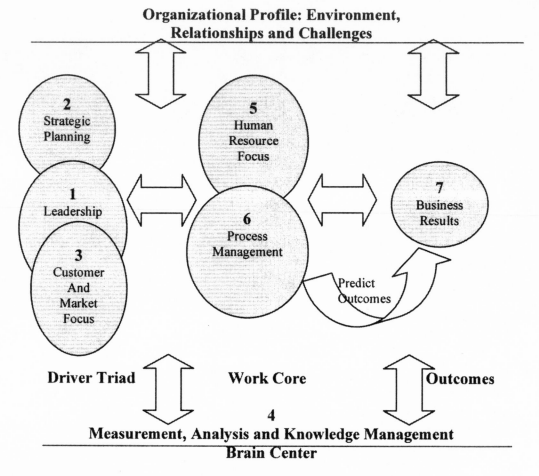

Figure 3.1 *The Framework of the Baldrige Criteria. Source: Adapted from Mark L. Blazey, Insights to Performance Excellence 2006.*

Category 2: Strategic Planning (85 points)

This category addresses how an organization develops strategic goals and objectives, action plans and human resource plans, and how quality and performance requirements are deployed (i.e., communicated, measured, and aligned) to all work units.

Category 3: Customer and Market Focus (85 points)

This category looks at the various ways that an organization builds and maintains strong and lasting relationships by meeting and exceeding customer and stakeholder requirements and expectations.

Category 4: Measurement, Analysis and Knowledge Management (90 points)

This category examines the different methods used by organizations in collecting and analyzing data and information to support performance improvements in customer satisfaction, products, services, and business processes. It also looks at how organizational knowledge is managed and transmitted throughout the entire organization.

Category 5: Human Resource Focus (85 points)

This category looks at how an agency enables employees to realize their full potential as they pursue the organization's quality objectives and performance goals.

Category 6: Process Management (85 points)

This category focuses on the use of systematic approaches in the design, management and improvement of value-creation (i.e., key business processes) and support processes.

Category 7: Business Results (450 points)

The results category considers the ways in which an organization's effectiveness and improvement trends are reflected in performance outcomes and performance levels relative to those of their competitors.

The Baldrige National Quality Award History

The Baldrige National Quality Award was created when President Ronald Reagan signed Public Law 100-107 on August 27, 1987. The award was named to honor Secretary of Commerce Malcolm Baldrige, who died in a rodeo accident in 1987. His transformational leadership contributed to significant improvements in process and outcome performance for the Department of Commerce, where he served from 1981 through 1987. During his tenure, he championed the use of quality principles to improve performance and helped draft an early version of the quality improvement act.

The purpose of the award, according to the National Standards of Science and Technology (Fact Sheet, 2005), is "to recognize U.S. organizations for their achievements in quality and performance and to raise awareness about the importance of quality and performance excellence as a competitive edge." Private and public businesses and industry, educational institutions, and health organizations have adopted the Baldrige Criteria, which have become the internationally recognized standards of performance excellence. In October 2004, President George W. Bush signed into law the legislation to expand the Baldrige Award to include government entities and non-profit agencies. Organizations use the Baldrige Criteria to assess their organizational climate, to deliver ever-improving products and services to customers, and to continuously improve performance.

The Findings and Purposes of Public Law 100–107 states

1. The leadership of the United States in product and process quality has been challenged strongly (and sometimes successfully) by foreign competition, and our Nation's productivity growth has improved less than our competitors' over the last two decades.

2. American business and industry are beginning to understand that poor quality costs companies as much as 20 percent of sales revenues nationally and that improved quality of goods and services goes hand in hand with improved productivity, lower costs, and increased profitability.

3. Strategic planning for quality and quality improvement programs, through a commitment to excellence in manufacturing and services, are becoming more and more essential to the well being of our Nation's economy and our ability to compete effectively in the global marketplace.

4. Improved management understanding of the factory floor, worker involvement in quality, and greater emphasis on statistical process control can lead to dramatic improvements in the cost and quality of manufactured products.

5. The concept of quality improvement is directly applicable to small companies as well as large, to service industries as well as manufacturing, and to the public sector as well as private enterprise.

6. In order to be successful, quality improvement programs must be management-led and customer-oriented, and this may require fundamental changes in the way companies and agencies do business.

7. Several major industrial nations have successfully coupled rigorous private-sector quality audits with national awards giving special recognition to those enterprises the audits identify as the very best; and

8. A national quality award program of this kind in the United States would help improve quality and productivity by:

    a. Helping to stimulate American companies to improve quality and productivity for the pride of recognition while obtaining a competitive edge through increased profits;

b. Recognizing the achievements of those companies that improve the quality of their goods and services and providing an example to others;

c. Establishing guidelines and criteria that can be used by business, industrial, governmental, and other organizations in evaluating their own quality improvement efforts; and

d. Providing specific guidance for other American organizations that wish to learn how to manage for high quality by making available detailed information on how winning organizations were able to change their cultures and achieve eminence.

The Baldrige National Quality Award Process

The Baldrige Award is a four-stage process that involves participation of the Board of Examiners and Panel of Judges (see Figure 3.2). At stage 1, an independent review of completed applications is conducted by members of the Board of Examiners. The Panel of Judges selects and recommends the top scoring applications for a consensus review, which is completed by the examiners at stage 2 of the process. The judges then select five finalists for a site visit review, which is conducted by the examiners. The purpose of the visit is to verify the accuracy of information provided, to clarify areas that are unclear, and to obtain additional data to resolve difference of opinions among examiners. During the final stage of the process, the judges review all the information provided by the examiners and recommend the Baldrige Award winners. The winners are announced during an annual ceremony held in Washington, D.C., typically in either October or November.

Why Apply for the Baldrige Award?

So why apply for this prestigious award? Why would you invest your precious resources on this approach? Listen to the "voice of the customers," who are far more persuasive than we are. Captured below are some of the comments from the 2002 applicants regarding the benefits of applying for the Baldrige Award. Note the high level of satisfaction among the applicants (Figure 3.3), as demonstrated by their willingness to recommend the process to other prospective applicants.

"Assessing our efforts against the Criteria, articulating our story, and preparing for the site visit were immensely valuable to our improvement efforts."

Overview of the Baldrige Award Process

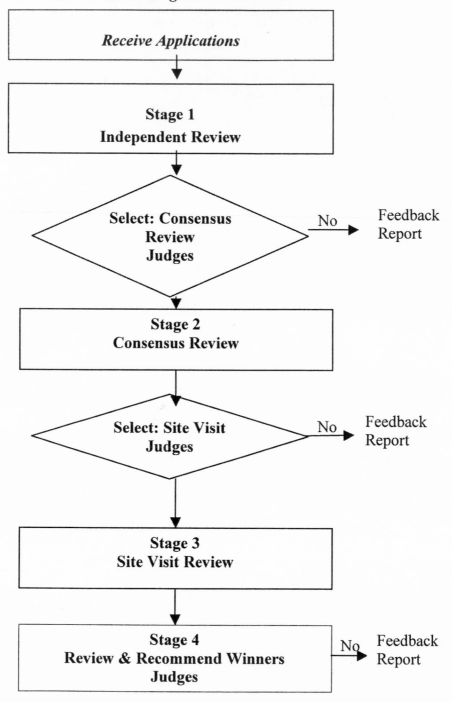

Figure 3.2 *Source: 2005 Baldrige National Quality Award Program.*

34

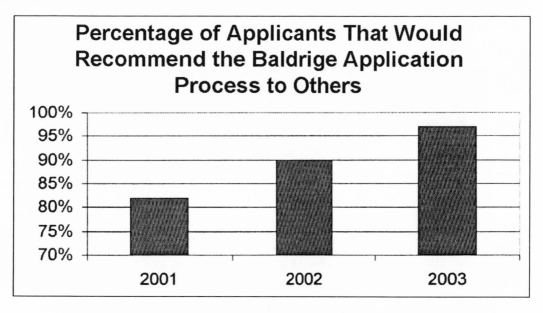

Percentage of Applicants That Would Recommend the Baldrige Application Process to Others

Figure 3.3 Source: 2005 Baldrige National Quality Program, "Why Apply?"

"We consult with other school districts about the Baldrige process and always emphasize the value of the application process."

"We credit the Malcolm Baldrige National Quality Award process as the key driver in achieving and sustaining our performance excellence results."

All applicants get a feedback report based on a comprehensive assessment of their completed applications and site visit reviews, if they qualify for the visit phase. The report is typically 50 pages long and includes the following key components: introduction to and background information on the application review process, key themes, Item level specifics of the applicant's Strengths and Opportunities for Improvements (OFIs), scoring summary of the applicant, and scoring distribution. The feedback report is intended to serve as a self-assessment tool, which could be the basis of the organization's improvement plans and action initiatives. The Baldrige National Quality Award Program publication "Why Apply?" provides the following description of the components of the feedback report:

- **Key Themes Summary**— A synthesis of the most significant, crosscutting strengths and opportunities for improvement in an organization's approaches and results provides a broad overview of the examiners' analyses.

- **Comments**— Actionable, detailed strengths and opportunities for improvement for each criteria Item, specific to an organization, help leaders prioritize improvement efforts.

- **Individual Scoring Range**—For each Item (or Category at stage 1), leaders will receive a 10 percent scoring range, allowing them to determine their organization's relative strengths and opportunities for improvement.
- **Scoring Distribution**—The percentage of applicants that scored in each of the eight scoring bands provides a context for an organization's score relative to other organizations.

Every year the staff of the Baldrige National Quality Award Program surveys all applicants to determine their level of satisfaction with the program and find out if the program meets their expectations. More than 80 percent of the respondents replied that they are either "very satisfied" or "satisfied" with the relevance of the feedback report to their efforts to continuously improve their processes, systems and performance (Figure 3.4). The value of the report relative to their investment is shown on Figure 3.5, where more than 80 percent expressed satisfaction with the return on their investment.

The Baldrige National Quality Award Criteria Structure and Questions

The seven Baldrige Quality *Criteria* are divided into *categories*, *items* and *areas to address*, as depicted in Figure 3.6. Each Category consists of two or more items,

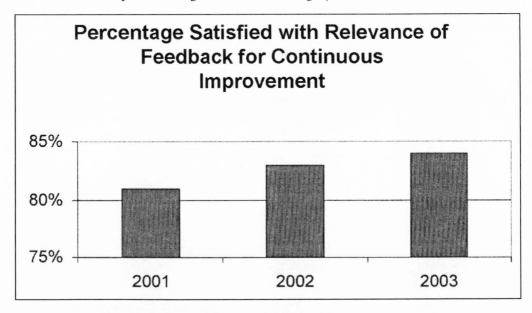

Figure 3.4 *Source: Baldrige National Quality Award Program.*

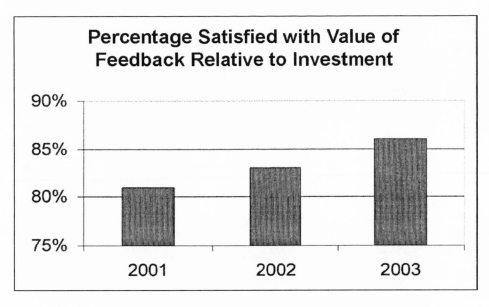

Figure 3.5 Source: Baldrige National Quality Award Program.

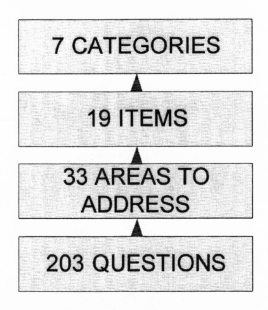

Figure 3.6 Baldrige Criteria Structure.

and each of the 19 items focus on a major requirement. Each Item consists of one or more areas to address for a total of 33. A detailed discussion of the 19 items and a sample application from a library are presented in Chapter 7, Interpreting and Using the Baldrige Criteria.

Table 3.1
Key Characteristics of the Baldrige Quality Criteria

Characteristics	Description
Directed toward business results	Organizational performance and results are a composite of the seven key performance areas.
Non-prescriptive	There are no requirements about how to implement the core values in a specific manner or the need to use any specific tools, techniques, technologies, systems or measures.
Supports goal-based diagnosis	The criteria focus on requirements while the scoring system focuses on factors to use in assessing strengths and areas for improvements.
Supports a system perspective and emphasizes alignment	Requires improvement cycles at all levels and and all parts of the organization. Strategic alignment is embedded in the cause and effect relationships and results orientation among all seven *Criteria*.
Comprehensive	The criteria cover all operations, processes and work units of the organizations, both internal and external.

Source: 2005 Baldrige National Quality Award Criteria

Approach, Deployment and Results

An important aspect of the scoring system is the weighing of points (the total score of which is 1000) among the seven categories. The scoring of responses to criteria items in the application and applicant feedback during the site visit is based on three evaluation dimensions: (1) Approach, (2) Deployment and (3) Results.

Approach refers to the methods and processes used by organizations in addressing the Baldrige Criteria Item requirements. Criteria 1 through 6 are evaluated on the approach and deployment dimensions. The approaches are evaluated on the following factors:

- Appropriateness of the methods and processes relative to the Item requirements
- The effectiveness of their use
- Alignment with organizational needs
- Evidence of beneficial innovation and change

Conceptually, the approach must be planned and implemented before deployment is possible.

Deployment refers to the extent to which the approach is applied to the criteria item requirements. The approaches must be deployed throughout the system — to all products and services, to all the different levels of the organization, and to both internal and external customers and stakeholders.

Results refer to effective outcomes in achieving the purposes of the Baldrige criteria item requirements. Item requirements for Category 7 are evaluated on results and the effectiveness of results is assessed using the following factors:

- Current performance
- The organization's performance compared to appropriate standards or benchmarks
- Rate and breadth of performance improvements
- Linkage of results measures to key customer, products, service requirements; process; and action plan performance identified in the organizational profile and in the approach-deployment items

	Table 3.2 **Scoring Guidelines for Processes**
Scores	*Processes (for use with CATEGORIES 1–6)*
0% or 5%	• No systematic approach is evident; information is anecdotal. (Alignment) • Little or no deployment of an approach is evident. (Deployment) • An improvement orientation is not evident; improvement is achieved through reacting to problems. (Learning) • No organizational alignment is evident; individual areas or work units operate independently. (Integration)
10%, 15%, **20%, or 25%**	• The beginning of a systematic approach to the basic requirements of the Item is evident. (A) • The approach is in the early stages of deployment in most areas or work units, inhibiting progress in achieving the basic requirements of the Item. (Deployment) • Early stages of a transition from reacting to problems to a general improvement orientation are evident. (Learning) • The approach is aligned with other areas or work units largely through joint problem solving. (Integration)
30%, 35%, **40%, or 45%**	• An effective, systematic approach, responsive to the basic requirements of the Item, is evident. (Alignment) • The approach is deployed, although some areas or work units are in early stages of deployment. (Deployment)

Table 3.2
Scoring Guidelines for Processes

Scores	Processes (for use with CATEGORIES 1–6)
	• The beginning of a systematic approach to evaluation and improvement of key processes is evident. (Learning) • The approach is in early stages of alignment with your basic organizational needs identified in response to the other Criteria Categories. (Integration)
50%, 55%, 60%, or 65%	• An effective, systematic approach, responsive to the overall requirements of the Item, is evident. (Alignment) • The approach is well deployed, although deployment may vary in some areas or work units. (Deployment) • A fact-based, systematic evaluation and improvement process and some organizational learning are in place for improving the efficiency and effectiveness of key processes. (Learning) • The approach is aligned with your organizational needs identified in response to the other Criteria Categories. (Integration)
70%, 75%, 80%, or 85%	• An effective, systematic approach, responsive to the multiple requirements of the Item, is evident. (Alignment) • The approach is well deployed, with no significant gaps. (Deployment) • Fact-based, systematic evaluation and improvement and organizational learning are key management tools; there is clear evidence of refinement and innovation as a result of organizational-level analysis and sharing. (Learning) • The approach is integrated with your organizational needs identified in response to the other Criteria Items. (Integration)
90%, 95%, or 100%	• An effective, systematic approach, fully responsive to the multiple requirements of the Item, is evident. (Alignment) • The approach is fully deployed without significant weaknesses or gaps in any areas or work units. (Deployment) • Fact-based, systematic evaluation and improvement and organizational learning are key organization-wide tools; refinement and innovation, backed by analysis and sharing, are evident throughout the organization. (Learning) • The approach is well integrated with your organizational needs identified in response to the other Criteria Items. (Integration)

Source: 2005 Baldrige National Quality Award Criteria

Table 3.3
Scoring Guidelines for Results

Scores	Results (for use with CATEGORY 7)
0% or 5%	• There are no business results or poor results in areas reported. • Trend data are either not reported or show mainly adverse trends. • Comparative information is not reported. • Results are not reported for any areas of importance to your organization's key business requirements.
10%, 15%, 20%, or 25%	• A few business results are reported; there are some improvements and/or early good performance levels in a few areas. • Little or no trend data are reported. • Little or no comparative information is reported. • Results are reported for a few areas of importance to your organization's key business requirements.
30%, 35%, 40%, or 45%	• Improvements and/or good performance levels are reported in many areas addressed in the Item requirements. • Early stages of developing trends are evident. • Early stages of obtaining comparative information are evident. • Results are reported for many areas of importance to your organization's key business requirements.
50%, 55%, 60%, or 65%	• Improvement trends and/or good performance levels are reported for most areas addressed in the Item requirements. • No pattern of adverse trends and no poor performance levels are evident in areas of importance to your organization's key business requirements. • Some trends and/or current performance levels — evaluated against relevant comparisons and/or benchmarks — show areas of good to very good relative performance. • Business results address most key customer, market, and process requirements
70%, 75%, 80%, or 85%	• Current performance is good to excellent in most areas of importance to the Item requirements. • Most improvement trends and/or current performance levels are sustained. • Many to most reported trends and/or current performance levels — evaluated against relevant comparisons and/or benchmarks — show areas of leadership and very good relative performance. • Business results address most key customer, market, process, and action plan requirements.

Table 3.3 Scoring Guidelines for Results	
Scores	*Results (for use with CATEGORY 7)*
90%, 95%, or 100%	• Current performance is excellent in most areas of importance to the Item requirements. • Excellent improvement trends and/or sustained excellent performance levels are reported in most areas. • Evidence of industry and benchmark leadership is demonstrated in many areas. • Business results fully address key customer, market, process, and action plan requirements.

Source: 2005 Baldrige National Quality Award Criteria

Quality Terminology

The following is a partial reprint of the Glossary of Terms from the 2005 Baldrige Business Criteria, published by the National Institute of Standards and Technology.

Action Plans

The term "action plans" refers to specific actions that respond to short- and long-term strategic objectives. Action plans include details of resource commitments and time horizons for accomplishment. Action plan development represents the critical stage in planning when strategic objectives and goals are made specific so that effective, organization-wide understanding and deployment are possible.

Alignment

The term "alignment" refers to consistency of plans, processes, information, resource decisions, actions, results, and analysis to support key organization-wide goals. Effective alignment requires a common understanding of purposes and goals. It also requires the use of complementary measures and information for planning, tracking, analysis, and improvement at three levels: the organizational level, the key process level, and the work unit level.

Analysis

The term "analysis" refers to an examination of facts and data to provide a basis for effective decisions. Analysis often involves the determination of cause and effect relationships. Overall organizational analysis guides the management of processes toward achieving key business results and toward attaining strategic objectives.

Anecdotal

The term "anecdotal" refers to process information that lacks specific methods, measures, deployment mechanisms, and evaluation/improvement/learning factors. Anecdotal information frequently uses examples and describes individual activities rather than systematic processes. An anecdotal response to how senior leaders deploy performance expectations might describe a specific occasion when a senior leader visited all company facilities. On the other hand, a systematic process might describe the communication methods used by all senior leaders to deliver performance expectations on a regular basis to all employee locations, the measures used to assess effectiveness of the methods, and the tools and techniques used to evaluate and improve the communication methods.

Approach

The term "approach" refers to the methods used by an organization to address the Baldrige Criteria item requirements. Approach includes the appropriateness of the methods to the Item requirements and the effectiveness of their use. Approach is one of the dimensions considered in evaluating *process items*.

Basic Requirements

The term "basic requirements" refers to the topic *criteria* users need to address when responding to the most central concept of an *Item*. Basic requirements are the fundamental theme of that Item (e.g., an approach for strategy development for Item 2.1). In the Criteria, the basic requirements of each Item are presented as the Item title.

Benchmarks

The term "benchmarks" refers to processes and results that represent best practices and performance for similar activities, inside or outside an organization's industry. Organizations engage in benchmarking to understand the current dimensions of world-class performance and to achieve discontinuous (non-incremental) or "breakthrough" improvement.

Customers

The term "customers" refers to actual and potential users of an organization's products or services. Customers include the end users of products or services, as well as others who might be the immediate purchasers of products or services, such as wholesale distributors, agents, or companies that further process an organization's product as a component of their product. The Criteria address customers broadly, referencing current customers, future customers, as well as customers of competitors.

Cycle Time

The term "cycle time" refers to the time required to fulfill commitments or to complete tasks. Time measurements play a major role in the Criteria because of the great importance of time performance to improving competitiveness. "Cycle time" also refers to all aspects of time performance. Cycle time improvement might include time to market, order fulfillment time, delivery time, changeover time, customer response time, and other key measures of time.

Deployment

The term "deployment" refers to the extent to which an approach is applied in addressing the requirements of a Baldrige Criteria Item. Deployment is evaluated on the basis of the breadth and depth of application of the approach to relevant work units throughout the organization. Deployment is one of the dimensions considered in evaluating process items.

Diversity

The term "diversity" refers to valuing and benefiting from personal differences. These differences may include race, religion, gender, nationality, physical or emotional disability, sexual orientation, age, education, geographic origin, and skill characteristics. Diversity can also mean differences in ideas, thinking, academic disciplines, and perspectives. The Baldrige Criteria refer to the diversity of an organization's employee hiring and customer communities.

Effective

The term "effective" refers to how well a process or a measure addresses its intended purpose. Determining effectiveness requires the evaluation of how well the approach is aligned with the organization's needs and the deployment of the approach, or the outcome of the measure used.

Empowerment

The term "empowerment" refers to giving employees the authority and responsibility to make decisions and take actions. Empowerment results in decisions being made closest to the "frontline," where work-related knowledge and understanding reside. Empowerment is aimed at enabling employees to satisfy customers on first contact, to improve processes and increase productivity, and to improve the organization's business results.

Ethical Behavior

The term "ethical behavior" refers to how an organization ensures that all its decisions, actions, and stakeholder interactions conform to the organization's moral and professional principles. These principles should support all applicable laws and regulations and are the foundation for the organization's culture and values.

Goals

The term "goals" refers to a future condition or performance level that one intends to attain. Goals are ends that guide actions. Goals can be both short- and long-term. Quantitative goals frequently referred to as "targets" include a numerical point or range. Targets might be projections based on comparative data or competitive data. The term "stretch goals" refers to desired major, discontinuous (non-incremental) or "breakthrough" improvements, usually in areas most critical to an organization's future success.

Governance

The term "governance" refers to the system of management and controls exercised in the stewardship of an organization. Governance processes may include approving strategic direction, monitoring and evaluating CEO performance, establishing executive compensation and benefits, succession planning, financial auditing, managing risk, disclosure, and shareholder reporting.

High-Performance Work

The term "high-performance work" refers to work processes used to systematically pursue ever higher levels of overall organizational and individual performance, including quality, productivity, innovation rate, and cycle time. High performance work results in improved service for customers and other stakeholders.

How

The term "how" refers to the processes that an organization uses to accomplish its mission requirements. In responding to "how" questions in the process item requirements, process descriptions should include information such as approach (methods and measures), deployment, learning, and integration factors.

Innovation

The term "innovation" refers to making meaningful change to improve products, services, processes, or organizational effectiveness, and to create new value for stakeholders. Innovation involves the adoption of an idea, process, technology, or product that is either new or new to its proposed application.

Integration

The term "integration" refers to the harmonization of plans, processes, information, resource decisions, actions, results, and analysis to support key organization-wide goals. Effective integration goes beyond alignment and is achieved when the individual components of a performance management system operate as a fully interconnected unit.

Key

The term "key" refers to the major or most important elements or factors that are critical to achieving your intended outcome. The Baldrige Criteria, for example, refer to key challenges, key plans, key processes, key measures — those that are most important to the organization's success.

Knowledge Assets

The term "knowledge assets" refers to the accumulated intellectual resources of an organization. It is the knowledge possessed by employees in the form of information, ideas, memory, insights, and cognitive and mechanical skills and capabilities.

Leadership System

The term "leadership system" refers to how leadership is exercised, formally and informally, throughout the organization — the basis for and the way key decisions are made, communicated, and carried out. It includes structures and mechanisms for decision-making, selection and development of leaders and managers, and reinforcement of values, ethical behavior, directions, and performance expectations.

Learning

The term "learning" refers to new knowledge or skills acquired through evaluation, study, experience, and innovation. The Baldrige Criteria include two distinct kinds of learning: organizational and personal. Organizational learning is achieved through research and development, evaluation and improvement cycles, employee and customer ideas and input, best practice sharing, and benchmarking. Personal learning is achieved through education, training, and developmental opportunities that further individual growth.

Levels

The term "levels" refers to numerical information that places or positions an organization's results and performance on a meaningful measurement scale. Performance levels permit evaluation relative to past performance, projections, goals, and appropriate comparisons.

Measures and Indicators

The term "measures and indicators" refers to numerical information that quantifies input, output, and performance dimensions of processes, products, services, and the overall organization (outcomes). Measures and indicators might be simple (derived from one measurement) or composite.

Mission

The term "mission" refers to the overall function of an organization. The mission answers the question, "What is this organization attempting to accomplish?" The mission might define customers or markets served, distinctive competencies, or technologies used.

Multiple Requirements

The term "multiple requirements" refers to the individual questions Criteria users need to answer within each Area to Address. These questions constitute the details of an *Item*'s requirements. They are presented in black text under each Item's Area(s) to Address.

Overall Requirements

The term "overall requirements" refers to the topics Criteria users need to address when responding to the central theme of an Item. Overall requirements address the most significant features of the Item requirements. In the Criteria, the overall requirements of each Item are presented in one or more introductory sentences printed in bold.

Partners

The term "partners" refers to those key organizations or individuals who are working in concert with an organization to achieve a common goal or to improve performance. Typically, partnerships are formal arrangements for a specific aim or purpose, such as to achieve a strategic objective or to deliver a specific product or service.

Performance

The term "performance" refers to output results and their outcomes obtained from processes, products, and services that permit evaluation and comparison relative to goals, standards, past results, and those of other organizations. Performance might be expressed in non-financial and financial terms.

Performance Projections

The term "performance projections" refers to estimates of future performance. Projections may be inferred from past performance, based on competitors' performance that must be met or exceeded, based on changes in a dynamic marketplace, or may be goals for future performance.

Process

The term "process" refers to linked activities with the purpose of producing a product or service for a user within or outside the organization. Generally, processes involve combinations of people, machines, tools, techniques, and materials in a defined series of steps or actions. In some situations, processes might require adherence to a specific sequence of steps, with documentation (sometimes formal) of procedures and requirements, including well-defined measurement and control steps.

Productivity

The term "productivity" refers to measures of the efficiency of resource use. Although the term often is applied to single factors such as staffing (labor productivity), machines, materials, energy, and capital, the productivity concept also applies to the total resources used in producing outputs.

Purpose

The term "purpose" refers to the fundamental reason that an organization exists. The primary role of purpose is to inspire an organization and to guide it in setting its values. Purpose is generally broad and enduring.

Results

The term "results" refers to outputs and outcomes achieved by an organization in addressing the requirements of a Baldrige Criteria Item. Results are evaluated on the basis of current performance; performance relative to appropriate comparisons; the rate, breadth, and importance of performance improvements; and the relationship of results measures to key organizational performance requirements.

Segment

The term "segment" refers to a part of an organization's overall customer, market, product line, or employee base. Segments typically have common characteristics that can be logically grouped. In results items, the term refers to disaggregating results data in a way that allows for meaningful analysis of an organization's performance.

Senior Leaders

The term "senior leaders" refers to an organization's senior management group or team. In many organizations, this consists of the head of the organization and his or her direct reports.

Stakeholders

The term "stakeholders" refers to all groups that are or might be affected by an organization's actions and success. Examples of key stakeholders include customers, employees, partners, governing boards, stockholders, suppliers, and local and professional communities.

Strategic Challenges

The term "strategic challenges" refers to those pressures that exert a decisive influence on an organization's likelihood of future success. These challenges frequently are driven by an organization's future competitive position relative to other providers of similar products or services.

Strategic Objectives

The term "strategic objectives" refers to an organization's articulated aims or responses to address major change or improvement, competitiveness issues, and business advantages. Strategic objectives generally are focused both externally and internally and relate to significant customer, market, product, service, or technological opportunities and challenges.

Sustainability

The term "sustainability" refers to an organization's ability to address current business needs and the agility and strategic management to prepare successfully for the future business and market environment. Both external and internal factors need to be considered.

Systematic

The term "systematic" refers to approaches that are well ordered, repeatable, and use data and information so learning is possible. In other words, approaches are systematic if they build in the opportunity for evaluation, improvement, and sharing, thereby permitting a gain in maturity.

Trends

The term "trends" refers to numerical information that shows the direction and rate of change for an organization's results. Trends provide a time sequence of organizational performance. A minimum of three data points is generally needed to begin to ascertain a trend. More data points are needed to define a statistically valid trend.

Value

The term "value" refers to the perceived worth of a product, service, process, or function relative to cost and to possible alternatives. Organizations need to understand what different stakeholder groups value and then deliver it to each group. This frequently requires balancing value for customers and other stakeholders, such as stockholders, employees, and the community.

Value Creation

The term "value creation" refers to processes that produce benefit for customers and for a business. They are the processes most important to "running your business"—those that involve the majority of employees and that generate products, services, and positive business results.

Values

The term "values" refers to the guiding principles and behaviors that embody how an organization and its people are expected to operate. Values support and guide the decision making of every employee, helping the organization to accomplish its mission. Examples of values might include showing integrity and fairness in all interactions, exceeding customer expectations, valuing employees and diversity, protecting the environment, and performance excellence every day.

Vision

The term "vision" refers to the desired future state of an organization. The vision describes where the organization is headed, what it intends to be, or how it wishes to be perceived in the future.

Work Systems

The term "work systems" refers to how your employees are organized into formal or informal units to accomplish an organization's mission and strategic objectives; how job responsibilities are managed; and processes for compensation, employee performance management, recognition, communication, hiring, and succession planning.

4

Starting a Quality Project: The Quality Management Plan

"The method of the enterprising is to plan with audacity and to execute with vigor."

— Christian Bovee

In this chapter, our attention will be focused on developing a systematic management plan to implement the Baldrige Criteria at all levels of the organization. There are eleven organizational (discrete) steps in this phase of the project, which are illustrated below:

Step 1: Top Management Commit to Quality & Provide Visible Leadership to Entire Organization

A fundamental requirement of any change effort involves top management's commitment to providing visible leadership, not only at the beginning but all throughout the process. Without top management's authentic involvement, the project will fail miserably. The top leaders must "walk the walk and talk the talk," not simply pay lip service to quality. They need to understand the concepts and principles of quality and their practical applications. They have to go through training, just like everyone involved in the project, which is the entire organization. They have to provide resources, both human capital and financial resources, to support the project for the long-term.

Senior leaders have to show strong leadership, identify and discuss the reasons for the change, examine major opportunities in adopting the Baldrige Criteria, and anticipate potential crises and consequences of keeping the status quo. They have

Quality Management Plan

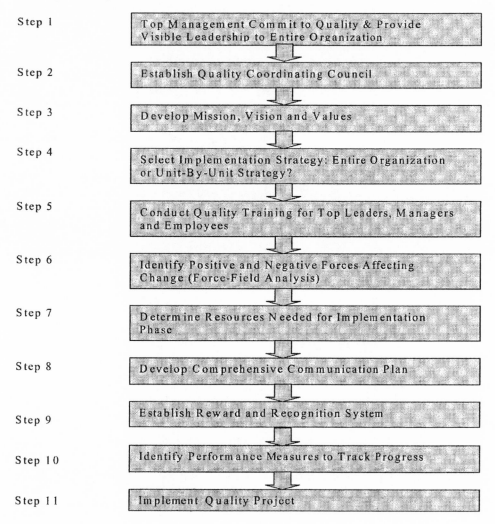

Step 1 — Top Management Commit to Quality & Provide Visible Leadership to Entire Organization

Step 2 — Establish Quality Coordinating Council

Step 3 — Develop Mission, Vision and Values

Step 4 — Select Implementation Strategy: Entire Organization or Unit-By-Unit Strategy?

Step 5 — Conduct Quality Training for Top Leaders, Managers and Employees

Step 6 — Identify Positive and Negative Forces Affecting Change (Force-Field Analysis)

Step 7 — Determine Resources Needed for Implementation Phase

Step 8 — Develop Comprehensive Communication Plan

Step 9 — Establish Reward and Recognition System

Step 10 — Identify Performance Measures to Track Progress

Step 11 — Implement Quality Project

to express their vision in compelling terms and be ready to lead, to achieve big and audacious goals. There will be tough times and good times, but leaders must be poised to motivate their employees to keep on going despite the challenges posed by the new and unfamiliar ways of doing things. After organizing the coordinating council, senior leaders have to participate at every key meeting and demonstrate their commitment to and knowledge of the Baldrige Criteria and where it will lead them. Employees need to be rewarded and little victories celebrated as the organization plows its way through unbroken grounds. When employees lose hope and courage, leaders have to be there to motivate them to forge ahead and go for the long haul. Everyone, both leaders and employees, needs to realize that the quality journey takes time — it's a long-term commitment, not a quick fix.

Step 2: Establish Quality Coordinating Council

Top leaders need to organize a group of dedicated and knowledgeable individuals to lead the quality effort and to provide an infrastructure for its continuous development. The organizations we worked with as consultants to implement a quality initiative identified quality team leaders and quality champions, and had a quality coordinator working with us.

Quality expert Dr. Mark L. Blazey noted in *Insights to Performance Excellence 2006*, "Quality champions are senior executives who work to improve leadership effectiveness." Their primary role is to lead "the entire organization towards developing a quality culture and becoming a quality organization." Quality team leaders are employees and middle managers who are knowledgeable in the area and serve as the link between top management and line employees in communicating the details of the quality effort to the workforce. They are the key individuals involved in working with employees as they design new processes and improve services. They also collaborate with other team members in writing the Baldrige application and in designing surveys and other quality improvement projects. The quality coordinator is the lead staff for the quality project and is the individual who plans, coordinates and monitors all activities related to the project, facilitates meetings, and monitors completion of the writing assignments for the Baldrige application.

The quality coordinating council typically consists of ten to twelve members from different departments and units, with representation from both leadership and the employee base. In essence, it is a cross-functional team, whose strength lies in its diversity of ideas and perspectives and its unity of purpose.

Step 3: Develop Mission, Vision and Values

What business are we in? What are our major reasons for existence? Where do we want to be three to five years from now? What type of organizational culture and values do we, the leaders, want to promote and nurture? What leadership and workforce competencies do we value and model? These are some of the internal questions that leaders and employees have to ask themselves before embarking on the quality journey. There has to be a clear and strong alignment between the culture of the organization and a quality culture. Without this critical link, improvements are bound to be incremental at best and, ultimately, temporary and fleeting. Sirota, Usilaner, and Weber (1994) conducted a comprehensive study of 30 companies to identify the critical dimensions which a corporate culture must possess in order to sustain a quality culture. Their findings are presented in table 4.1 below.

Table 4.1 Elements of a Quality Culture	
ELEMENTS	*DESCRIPTIONS*
Focus on excellence	Commitment to being the best
Focus on customers	Knowledge of and responsiveness to customer requirements
Employee orientation	Organization trusts employees and cares about them
Sense of direction	Clear strategic direction
Fact-based decision making	Use of internal data and external benchmarks
Continuous improvement	Belief that status quo is unsatisfactory
Collaboration	Cooperation among team, across functions
Open communication	Information shared in all directions
Empowerment	Employees can make changes affecting their jobs
Reward and recognition	Incentives are non-monetary and monetary
Training and development	Employees have access to development skills
Corporate/organizational citizenship	Ethical, community-oriented management

Source: Sirota, Usilaner and Weber, "Sustaining Quality Improvement" (1994)

Step 4: Select Implementation Strategy: Entire Organization or Unit-By-Unit Strategy?

Senior leaders have to make a decision on an implementation strategy. Which option is more appropriate: implementing quality for the entire organization or selecting a pilot unit? The incremental approach might be better for large organizations in which departments have different levels of quality readiness. This

Figure 4.1 *Alignment between Organizational Culture and Quality Culture.*

approach also enables change makers to apply the learnings from the pilot project to the other departments.

When making this key decision, leaders have to consider several factors such as organizational culture, quality readiness, competencies, resources, and other internal and external factors.

Step 5: Conduct Quality Training for Top Leaders, Managers and Employees

It is recommended that training start with the top leaders, who have to demonstrate visible and continuing commitment to the quality project. Training should include a comprehensive curriculum on the principles and philosophy of quality and their application to libraries, and an overview of basic quality improvement tools. Line managers and employees, who have to implement the project, would need a more comprehensive and in-depth training on the principles of quality, the Baldrige Quality Criteria and quality improvement tools (basic and advanced). Leaders and managers who have the aptitude and the motivation to engage in additional training might be encouraged to become Baldrige quality examiners, which would provide them with advance and expert training in the principles and application of quality. It is also highly recommended that the entire organization engage in a change management workshop to better equip everyone to navigate the unpredictable and unfamiliar landscape of transition and change.

Step 6: Identify Positive and Negative Forces Affecting Change (Force-Field Analysis)

As part of the change management workshop, the leaders and employees have to engage in an honest discussion of the positive and negative forces affecting the transition to a new management system. The purpose of this intervention is to address the barriers to change and to do more of what is working in order to facilitate the transition to a new operating model. This technique is discussed in greater detail on page 71, following the section on quality improvement tools.

Step 7: Determine Resources Needed for Implementation Phase

Before the formal launching of the quality project, it would be useful for the quality coordinating committee to draft a Gantt chart outlining all the core tasks that need to be completed, the resources that need to be lined up, the lead staff that need to be involved and the time needed for completion. Addressing all these key issues could eliminate a lot of minor operational glitches, which cumulatively could become major barriers to progress.

Step 8: Develop Comprehensive Communication Plan

In *Communicating for Change* (1996), Roger D'Aprix urges "change agents to re-create communication as a management system by developing the four key elements of strategy, accountability, rewards and trainings (dust jacket)." He contends that internal communications need to be guided by a planned strategy, a clear accountability for the type of behavior that is necessary to support the strategy, a reward system to reinforce the desired behavior and systematic training to make the accountability enforceable. He points out that we have systems for most of our core and support functions, such as human resource, technology, financial, administrative, to name a few, so why not one for communication? Increasing the importance of this leadership role could very well be the key to avoiding communication breakdowns that occur often in today's workplace. In an information society, where change is constant, knowledge workers need to be armed with up-to-date information to understand what is happening and why.

Change agents and leaders need to use every form of communication to share the new vision, develop an operating model and teach new competencies and behaviors. The challenge, D'Aprix declared, "is to develop messages that further people's understanding, commitment and productivity." Strategic communication requires an effort on the part of leaders to connect the organization's mission and vision with the requirements of the customers, which are constantly changing. As leaders, we need to provide employees with the "what and why" of quality, how it affects our mission and how it impacts their work. Knowledge of this clear alignment and its critical role in the equation could give meaning and value to employees' work. Instead of laboring like cyborgs, workers can now be engaged stakeholders in their own workplace.

Step 9: Establish Reward and Recognition System

Rewarding and recognizing contributions in the quality program, for both teams and individuals, could go a long way in sustaining commitment for the journey ahead. Incentives could include non-monetary rewards, such as recognition plaques and certificates (e.g., outstanding quality project award or customer service award), special parking spaces, gift certificates, release time, special assignments and trips, to name just a few.

Step 10: Identify Performance Measures to Track Progress

A simple monitoring instrument could be developed to track the progress of the quality implementation plan. For instance, Gantt chart could be used to track milestones, lead staff and timelines. It's always a good idea to track progress so that adjustments can be made mid-way during the process, if planned activities are not working or if objectives are unrealistic.

Step 11: Implement Quality Project

Now that we have a solid plan and have laid the groundwork for success, we're ready to start the implementation phase. Get set for a seven-step process. In the next chapter, we will apply what we have learned about the Baldrige Criteria not simply to win an award but to continuously improve performance excellence. In this phase, we conduct a preliminary self-assessment and act on the findings; identify our customers, key processes and performance measures; and apply the Baldrige Criteria to all levels of the organization. Next we will benchmark our performance outcomes, monitor and evaluate results and act on the findings of our monitoring and evaluation process.

5

Putting the Plan into Action: Quality Implementation

"Whatever you can do, or dream you can, begin it. Boldness has genius, power, and magic in it."
— Goethe (1749–1832)

Step 12: Complete Self Assessment

It's always a good idea to start the quality journey by determining an organization's readiness for quality. This could be done even before applying for the National Baldrige Quality Award or its local state counterpart to give leaders an overview of where the organization is in the quality spectrum. Below is a sample self-analysis worksheet from the Baldrige National Quality Program *2006 Criteria for Performance Excellence* booklet. The same format could be followed for the remaining six categories.

SAMPLE: Baldrige Application Self-Analysis Worksheet (Optional)

While insights gained from external examiners or reviewers are always helpful, leaders know their organizations better than anyone else does and are in an excellent position to identify key strengths and key opportunities for improvement (OFIs). Having just completed the Baldrige Criteria questions, leaders can accelerate improvement journey by doing a self-analysis.

Instructions:

Use this optional worksheet to list your key strengths and key OFIs. Start by identifying one or two strengths and one or two OFIs for each Criteria category. For those of high importance, establish a goal and a plan of action.

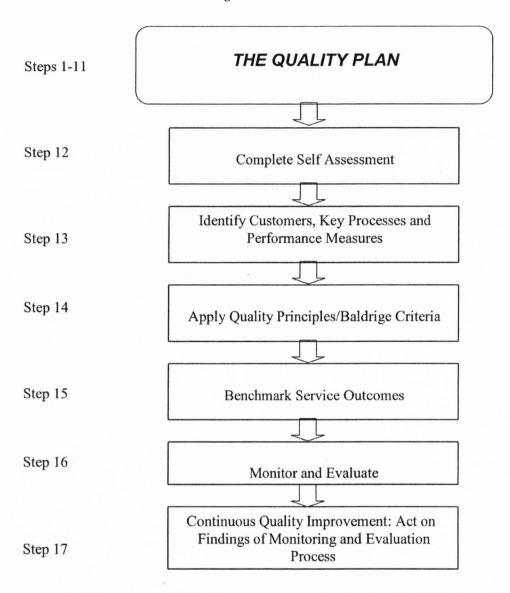

Steps 1-11	**THE QUALITY PLAN**
Step 12	Complete Self Assessment
Step 13	Identify Customers, Key Processes and Performance Measures
Step 14	Apply Quality Principles/Baldrige Criteria
Step 15	Benchmark Service Outcomes
Step 16	Monitor and Evaluate
Step 17	Continuous Quality Improvement: Act on Findings of Monitoring and Evaluation Process

Step 13: Identify Customers, Key Processes and Performance Measures

An initial conversation that must happen among leaders, the quality coordinating council members and a representative group of employees is the identification of customers and stakeholders, key processes and performance measures. The first two areas have to be addressed before applying for the Baldrige National Quality

Criteria Category	Importance High, Medium, Low	For High-Importance Areas			
		Stretch (Strength) or Improvement (OFI) Goal	What Action Is Planned?	By When?	Who Is Responsible?
OFI					
1.					
2.					

Criteria Category	Importance High, Medium, Low	For High-Importance Areas			
		Stretch (Strength) or Improvement (OFI) Goal	What Action Is Planned?	By When?	Who Is Responsible?
Category 1—Leadership					
Strength					
1.					
2.					

Award, which as we indicated is also designed to provide leaders with a comprehensive assessment of performance effectiveness in the seven quality *criteria*.

Step 14: Apply Quality Principles/ Baldrige Criteria

After completing the initial internal assessment of the organizational climate and the application for the Baldrige National Quality Award, it is time to apply the principles and criteria at the organizational or unit level. At the organizational level, the application and improvements cascade down from the organization to the smaller organizational units, whereas in the unit pilot project, applications migrate from one selected unit to another.

Step 15: Benchmark Service Outcomes

How do leaders know that the goals they set for their organization are good goals? Are they stretch goals, big, hairy and audacious goals, or simply maintenance goals? The quality way tells us to compare our goals and performance to those of our competitors or those who are the best in the business. To do that companies often employ benchmarking, a method for comparing processes or results that represent the best practices and performance for similar entities or activities. Competitors should be used as benchmarks only if they are the best in the business. Businesses in dissimilar industries or agencies with similar processes might be a better benchmarking choice for organizations trying to make breakthrough improvements in their processes.

The benchmarking process gained popularity in 1979, when the Xerox Corporation pioneered it to improve processes and products. At that time, Xerox was facing strong competition from Japanese manufacturers such as Canon, Minolta and Ricoh. They benchmarked their costs, materials and parts, and manufacturing process against the Japanese competitors. After Xerox developed a formal process to implement benchmarking, other large corporations followed their lead. Helene-Curtis, AT&T, DuPont and General Motors, to name a few, employed benchmarking to improve business strategies rather than relying on processes and products.

The following figure describes the benchmarking method jointly developed by Boeing, Digital, Motorola and Xerox. The rows on the left describe what activities need to be performed within the organization. The rows on the right depict the best practices of the organization being benchmarked.

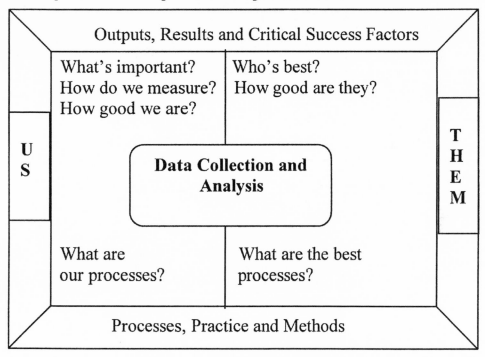

Figure 5.1 *Benchmarking Process. Source: Xerox, Competitive Benchmarking (1988).*

Step 16: Monitor and Evaluate

There is ample evidence supporting the need to monitor and to evaluate any intervention, especially during the implementation phase. What gets evaluated gets done, and what gets monitored gets done well. Monitoring provides the program implementer with the opportunity to modify steps, activities and projects mid-way through the process, thus using resources in the most cost-effective ways and enhancing the quality of outcomes.

Accountability is a major driver in efforts to evaluate program effectiveness, in addition to the need to continuously improve the program, which is an equally important consideration.

Step 17: Continuous Quality Improvement: Act on Findings of Monitoring and Evaluation Process

This is the final step of the process, which when deployed adds depth and value to the findings of the evaluation and monitoring process. It is the ultimate phase of the PDSA process, the Act Phase, where all the opportunities for improvements and the learnings from the past couple of months are applied to improve the processes, procedures and outcomes of the quality project implementation.

6

Maintaining and Improving Your Commitment to the Baldrige Criteria

"The secret of success is constancy of purpose."
— Benjamin Disraeli
(1804–1881)

Quality Involves a Change in Culture

How do organizations sustain the quality improvements that they have worked hard to achieve? How do they continuously improve on the gains of the last couple of years? As we noted earlier, quality requires a cultural change and only organizations that align their culture and values with the quality principles succeed. Sirota, Usilaner and Weber studied the factors that are critical for continued organizational success; their findings were published in the article "Sustaining Quality Improvements" in the March-April 1994 issue of *The Total Quality Review*. According to the authors, the strongest proof of the critical link between quality management success and corporate culture could be found among the Baldrige National Quality Award winners, including Corning, Federal Express, IBM Rochester and Motorola.

All of the award winners made significant changes in their cultures, which in turn resulted in enduring organizational and individual behavioral change (i.e., more than the typical three-year shelf-life). We are indebted to the authors for allowing us to share the results of their study. The following is a complete list of the fundamental changes in culture that they outlined as prerequisites to success:

- Visible, unquestionable leadership that focuses the entire organization on the cultural change about to take place (including raising people's awareness about a projected crisis if business continues as is)

- An effort to identify barriers to the cultural change, and development of action plans to overcome these barriers
- A set of quality values and goals (e.g., exceeding customers' expectations) to guide the business
- A comprehensive communication plan to cascade the value to every level of the company
- A mechanism to encourage management commitment at every level to the changes about to be made, as well as the newly established goals
- A reward and recognition system that reinforces the values and the goals of the new culture
- Training programs designed to equip employees with the skills necessary for quality improvement
- A measurement system to track progress (including employee and customer surveys to determine how well the new values have been incorporated)

Quality Management Do's and Don'ts

The following list is reprinted from the U.S. Department of Transportation's *Lessons Learned: Getting Started/Revitalizing Your TQM Effort*, a publication made up of do's and don'ts from various federal agencies.

Do's

- Do capitalize on previous experiences and lessons learned
- Do act in concert, not unilaterally
- Do keep the organizational mission, rather than turf, in the forefront
- Do see yourself as a leader of change
- Do invest "up front" to get results "down the road" (IRS Ogden Service Center)
- Do keep the message simple and uncomplicated
- Do make use of communication opportunities to reinforce quality
- Do concentrate on attitude instead of tools and techniques in the beginning
- Do generate champions, using early project teams (Social Security Administration)
- Do it, don't study it to death
- Do involve middle managers early on
- Do involve unions early in the process (Department of Interior)

- Do build quality into the system; this is the key to continuity (Internal Revenue Service)
- Do interject quality improvements in government documents that may appear unrelated (Department of Commerce)
- Do tailor training to fit your organization's needs
- Do include input from customers in setting your course of direction and in prioritizing activities (Army Aviation System's Command)

Don'ts

- Don't call it quality management if you don't want to, but do quality management
- Don't expect much and you won't be disappointed. Plan what you are going to do, but don't plan so carefully that you never get started (Federal Lands Highway)
- Don't force one approach on all federal level organizations (Department of Interior)
- Don't view quality management as a short-term fix
- Don't require bureaucratic approvals for quality initiatives; it stifles the process (Department of Commerce)
- Don't have training that is long on philosophy and short on application of concepts, tools, and disciplined problem solving (Army Aviation Systems Command)
- Don't loose sight of your organization's mission. This is often the most obvious characteristic of a true bureaucracy
- Don't concentrate on statistical process control in the beginning-work on attitudes (Social Security Administration)

Some Useful Quality Improvement Tools

In this section, we will discuss and demonstrate the practical applications of some basic quality improvement tools. They are useful in analyzing problems, continually improving processes, involving employees in the analysis of data and work processes, and using data to support decision-making.

Brainstorming

Brainstorming is a technique used by a team to creatively and efficiently generate ideas for solving problems and issues by creating an environment that is free of judgment and criticism.

Cause and Effect or Fishbone Diagram

This is a process that examines cause and effect relationships and possible root causes of problems by portraying possible causes in a graph.

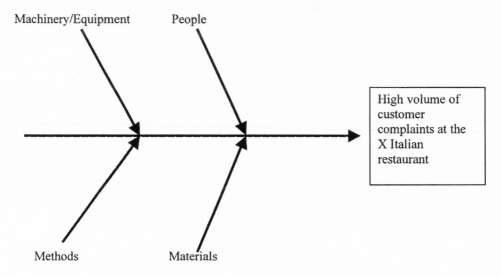

Figure 6.1 *Fishbone Diagram*

Flowchart

A flowchart describes the sequence of events in a process to enable the team to analyze the relative importance of each step. It allows the participants to design a new process or to modify the existing one. The figure below charts the complaint management process of Delaware Division of Libraries.

Bar Chart

A bar chart shows a comparison of quantities by graphically portraying them in the length of the bars. The example below displays the percentage of library patrons who speak languages other than English at home. Note that a clear majority is in the younger age group (0–14).

Pareto Chart

A Pareto Chart identifies the significant factors in a subject or problem being analyzed by showing their frequency size in a descending bar graph. It is based on the

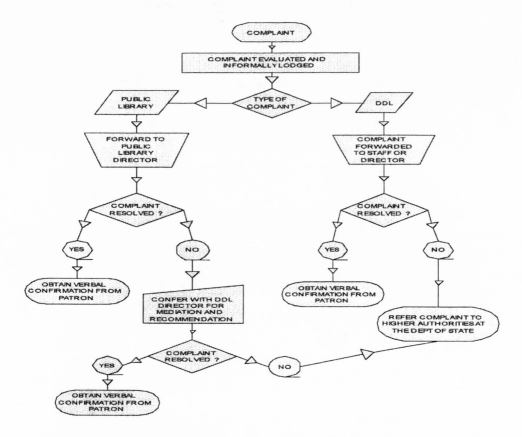

Figure 6.2 *Complaint Management Process of a State Library for Using a Flowchart.*

empirically validated principle that 20 percent (the vital few) of the source causes 80 percent (the trivial many) of the problem, which was developed by sociologist Wilfredo Pareto. Figure 6.4 is an example of the use of the Pareto Chart in displaying the major reasons why citizens of a community do not use their local library.

Control Chart

Control charts are used to assess an ongoing process over a period of time by analyzing variations and their causes. The purpose of the analysis is to control process variations and stabilize fluctuations within acceptable and predictable limits in order to improve quality, reduce cost and increase productivity.

Force-Field Analysis

This is a technique that looks at the positives (driving forces) and negatives (restraining forces) of a situation, an issue or a problem so that the positive forces

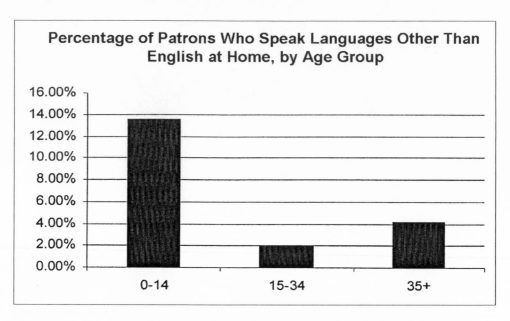

Figure 6.3 *Percentage of Patrons Who Speak Language Other Than English at Home, by Age Group. Bar Chart.*

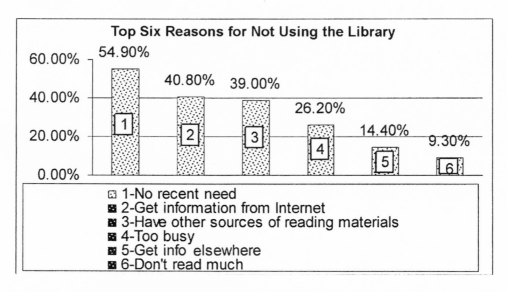

Figure 6.4 *Top Six Reasons for Not Using the Library. Pareto Chart.*

can be reinforced and the negative forces eliminated or minimized. This process is often used in assessing the forces affecting organizational change. The factors are typically portrayed in a two-column table, listing both negative and positive forces in descending importance and frequency. For example, in Table 6.1, private University XYZ is attempting to increase enrollment and compete effectively with other postsecondary institutions in the tri-state area. Its goal is to be recognized as the best institution in the area and to increase enrollment by 10 percent annually for the next five years.

Outlined below are the positive forces driving change and the competing negative forces restraining the achievement of the goal. The students rated the factors on a scale of 1 to 5, with 1 representing the weakest force and 5 representing the strongest force.

Table 6.1 Force-Field Analysis	
Positive Forces +	*Negative Forces* -
Low tuition +5	Enrollment process: inefficient; takes too long; untrained staff; too many forms -5
Trained and experienced educators +5	Limited financial aid -5
Flexible class schedules +5	Not enough parking spaces -4
Open enrollment +5	Classrooms need repair; too small; too cold during winter & too hot during summer -4
On-line and blended learning +4 State-of-the art technology +4	
TOTAL +28	-18

An analysis of the positive and negative forces indicates that there are stronger positive forces supporting the pursuit of the goal (i.e., to be recognized as the best postsecondary institution in the tri-state area) when compared with the negative forces. Our recommendation is for the leaders and the employees to do more of what works best and to remove or minimize the barriers to change. In other words, address the negative forces vigorously and you'll remove the major bottleneck to change.

PDSA (Plan, Do, Study, Act) Cycle

The PDSA cycle is a sequence of repeatable steps that may be applied to any improvement activity or project. The original concept of Plan, Do, Check, Act (PDCA) was developed by Walter Shewhart, a statistician at Bell Laboratories. Shewhart used the process to provide an analytical framework for the design of experiments. W.E. Deming introduced the concept to the Japanese innovators as the Plan, Do, Study, Act (PDSA).

Figure 6.6 describes the PDSA process used by the senior leaders of a state library system in setting and developing the organization's strategic plan. During the plan phase, leaders conduct a SWOT (strengths, weaknesses, opportunities and threats) analysis

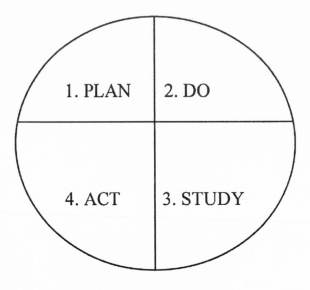

Figure 6.5 The PDSA Cycle.

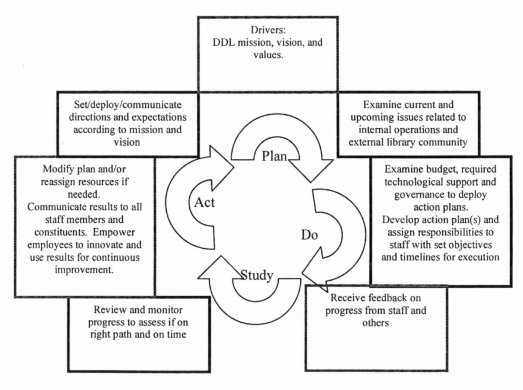

Figure 6.6 How Senior Leaders Set, Deploy and Communicate the Library's Strategic Plan Using the PDSA Cycle.

of both the internal and external environments. They review the budget and other needed resources before drafting a strategic action plan. During the do phase, they develop and draft a strategic plan, aligned with the agency's mission, vision, and values.

During the study phase, the leadership solicits feedback from customers, employees and stakeholders to assess the integrity of the plan. During the act phase, the plan is modified based on both internal and external feedback and the results are then communicated to all the employees, managers, and stakeholders.

Employees and management are empowered to implement the changes and to continuously improve processes in order to exceed customer satisfaction. The circular PDSA process illustrated above is repeated annually to maintain performance excellence and exceed performance standards.

7

Interpreting and Using
the Baldrige Criteria

"Knowledge is power."
— Francis Bacon
(1561–1626)

What Do These Criteria Mean?

Up until this chapter, we have done nothing except applaud the Baldrige Criteria and their application as superior to any other approach to performance improvement for organizations. We purposely did not tell you about the problems with the system until we had convinced you that it is a worthy gamble, in terms of time, energy and expenditure. The major drawback of the approach is the way the Criteria and the questions are written. They are written in "Greek" and an interpreter is needed to translate the questions to English. There is a certain mystique to it, but once the "secret" is uncovered, the magic unfolds. In this section of Chapter 7, we will do our level best to speak in plain, simple and clear language so you can begin to understand the basic tenets of this profoundly effective method.

This journey toward the "Eureka!" moment of understanding the Baldrige Way is a bit like the challenges faced by Sisyphus, the king of Corinth in Greek mythology, who incurred the wrath of Zeus. He was punished by having to push a big rock uphill, but the rock always rolled back on him. There is, however, a slight difference: with the Baldrige, the more you know, the easier it gets. You can push that proverbial rock uphill! Take heed, though. The Baldrige journey is not for the meek; it takes time and a considerable investment of human and financial resources. But once you are convinced of its usefulness and efficacy, you will be addicted to a way of life that you have not experienced before. The quest for excellence is a long and never-ending journey.

In this section, we will attempt to explain what the category items mean and provide examples gleaned from our experiences working with governmental agencies and non-profit organizations. We will also share what high-performing organizations do to comply with and to excel in these 19 items. So, let us begin this voyage of discovery.

Category 1: Leadership (90 points)

The leadership category addresses ways in which senior leaders create and sustain a customer-focused quality culture that values empowerment, innovation, learning and public responsibility.

Strong and empowering leaders with a compelling vision of where they intend to lead the organization are critical ingredients for high-performing organizations. This category asks how senior leaders define their mission and future vision, how they promote ethical behavior, and how they create a culture that values performance improvement.

1.1 Senior Leadership (70 pts.) Process

Describe HOW SENIOR LEADERS guide and sustain your organization. Describe HOW SENIOR LEADERS communicate with employees and encourage high PERFORMANCE.

What Does This Item Mean?

This Item asks you, the senior leaders, to define the mission, vision, and direction of your organization, and the key values that guide your organization. It asks you to describe the process you use in setting your mission, vision, and values.

Typically, these tasks are done through a strategic planning process. If a traditional strategic planning process is followed, the senior team and a small representative group of employees comprise the planning team. Another alternative is to use a large group intervention, where nearly everyone in the agency participates. Or it can involve a sizeable group of employees representing different functional areas and demographic profiles. For example, Ben & Jerry's Homemade Ice Cream holds its meetings at company picnics, where all the stakeholders and their families are invited to participate. A government agency where we worked as consultants involved a representative sample of employees and all the division directors in the planning sessions. It does not matter what process you use as long as it is a structured and consistent process. What do we mean by this? It simply means that there are consistent steps you follow at a projected time, such as annually or bi-annually. It could follow a structured process, such as the one displayed on page 78.

This Item also asks you to tell the examiners and the judges how you communicate your mission, your vision, and organizational values to your customers, employees, and other stakeholders. Some of the types of communication used by public agencies we worked with include verbal communications, such as town meetings, breakfast chats and retreats, and written communications, such as newsletters, weekly reports, e-mail messages, and special communiqués.

This Item also asks you to describe how you set your values. Do you involve your senior leaders and get feedback from your employees and council members? Or do you draft it yourself, sitting quietly in your plush high-rise office? It does not really matter how you do it, as long as you get buy-in from your leaders, employees and stakeholders. The key is to obtain their input and to clearly communicate the final product. More important, the values need to support your mission and vision and should be reflected in your actions. Values are reflected in what you do, not in what you say.

Finally, the leadership category focuses your attention on how you encourage superior performance by looking at your organizational structure. Are there layers of bureaucratic approvals before decisions are made or are employees encouraged to make decisions on how to do their jobs? Are employees made accountable for the results? Does your structure impede or encourage speed, agility and innovation? For example, we worked with a state division where the employment counselors led the streamlining efforts to improve their key work process. They meet monthly as a team, charged with the responsibility and armed with the authority to improve processes, methods, and operations within their units.

1.2 Governance and Social Responsibilities (50 pts.) Process

Describe your organization's GOVERNANCE system. Describe HOW your organization addresses its responsibilities to the public, ensures ETHICAL BEHAVIOR, and practices good citizenship.

What Does This Item Mean?

This Item asks you to describe how you make sure that your agency has a systematic mechanism to protect public safety, to ensure integrity and honesty among leaders and employees, and to promote corporate citizenship. Are there clear rules and regulations communicated to the workforce that define acceptable and ethical behavior? Is there an external body that oversees compliance with the regulations and provides feedback when lines are crossed? In most state and local governments, there are merit rules that define hiring, selection, promotion and discipline. When rules are violated, there are regulatory bodies that review and render decisions. For example, in Delaware state government, we have the Personnel Commission that reviews violations of Merit Rules; the Auditor's Office that reviews financial transactions; and the Public Integrity Commission that ensures ethical behavior among public servants. In addition to issuing rules of conduct and behavior, these governing entities provide feedback as to how organizations may prevent future violations or address and rectify current ones. Failure to comply with the rules or legal mandates could result in fines, penalties and other legal consequences, which are designed to control behavior that fall outside acceptable boundaries.

This Item on governance and social responsibility emerged in reaction to the financial scandals caused by big corporate violators such as Enron, Arthur Anderson, and WorldCom.

Category 2: Strategic Planning (85 points)

This category addresses how an organization develops strategic goals and objectives, action plans and human resource plans, and how quality and performance requirements are deployed to all work units. It also examines how your strategic objectives and action plans are deployed and changed, if circumstances require, and how progress is measured.

2.1 Strategy Development (40 pts.) Process
Describe HOW your organization establishes its strategy and STRATEGIC OBJECTIVES, including HOW you address your STRATEGIC CHALLENGES. Summarize your organization's KEY STRATEGIC OBJECTIVES and their related GOALS.

What Does This Item Mean?

This Item asks you to describe the process you use in defining your strategic objectives and goals, which are components of your strategic planning process. It is an extension of the leaders' role of defining what business you are in (mission) and what future direction they envision leading the organization (Step 1). Figure 7.1 illustrates a typical strategic planning process which we have used in our consulting practice.

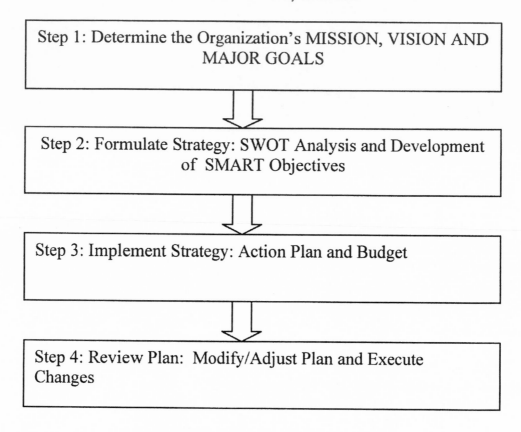

Figure 7.1 Four Stages of the Planning Process.

Step 1: Determine the Organization's Mission, Vision and Major Goals

Most strategic plans have both a vision and mission statement. Some also have a preamble that sets an agency tone. Others have a set of principles, an operating philosophy, even a history so that people have an organizational context. In short, this is the "purpose" element of the plan. All of the above is often captured in a single page.

Step 2: Formulate Strategy: SWOT Analysis and Development of SMART Objectives

Once the mission and vision are agreed upon, leaders guide the organization in selecting appropriate strategies to accomplish its mission and to achieve its goals.

In addition to goals, SMART (Specific, Measurable, Achievable, and Time-Related) objectives and strategies are also formulated. During this phase leaders and employees attempt to answer the fundamental question: "What do we want to do in order to successfully achieve our mission and get us closer to our vision?"

It is also during this phase that leaders and employees engage in a SWOT (Strength, Weaknesses, Opportunities, and Threats) analysis.

2.2 Strategy Deployment (45 pts.) Process

Describe HOW your organization converts its STRATEGIC OBJECTIVES into ACTION PLANS. Summarize your organization's ACTION PLANS and related KEY PERFORMANCE MEASURES or INDICATORS. Project your organization's future PERFORMANCE on these KEY PERFORMANCE MEASURES or INDICATORS.

What Does This Item Mean?

This Item is a continuation of the strategic planning process in Item 2.1 and involves the development of action plans, complete with measures, targets, and timeliness (steps 3 and 4 of Figure 7.1). Below is a discussion of what typically occurs during the strategy deployment phase.

Step 3: Implement Strategy: Action Plan and Budget

After reaching consensus on the appropriate strategies and objectives to achieve the organization's mission and vision, leaders and employees face the challenge of executing the plan. This is the stage where a majority of organizations fail. The problem is that too many plans are not really strategic — they do not have an implementation strategy as a component, nor does leadership actually take guidance from the plan. In other words, the plan is more of a compliance document than a blueprint for action and is filed away promptly after its completion.

In order to increase the strategic plan's role in establishing the organization's mission and charting its future direction, participants need to draft an action plan, which could include the following steps: allocate responsibility to a lead staff or team; identify needed resources; define realistic timelines for completion; and specify what initiatives and methods will be used to implement the strategies.

Step 4: Review Plan: Modify/Adjust Plan and Execute Changes

During the final phase, management and staff review the plan and assess what modifications and changes have to be made to adjust to the changing internal and external environments. By definition, strategic plans have a longer time horizon than operational plans; therefore, reviewing the plan annually is of critical importance. In today's information and high-tech society, there are rapid changes in the external environment that affect the way we do business. High-performing organizations do not "lock in" strategic goals and objectives for three to five years without periodically reviewing their relevance to the achievement of agency mission and future direction. After adjusting and modifying plans, action plans are executed and performance outcomes are measured.

Finally, the strategy development Item asks how your projected performance for your short-term and long-term planning horizons compares with those of your competitors. You are also asked to provide details on your projected performance and past performance as compared with those of your competitors or comparable organizations.

Category 3: Customer and Market Focus (85 points)

This category looks at the various ways that an organization builds and maintains strong and lasting relationships with customers by meeting and exceeding customer and stakeholder requirements and expectations.

3.1 Customer and Market Knowledge (40 pts.) Process

Describe HOW your organization determines requirements, expectations, and preferences of CUSTOMERS and markets to ensure the continuing relevance of your products and services and to develop new opportunities.

What Does This Item Mean?

Because customers are central to the survival of most organizations, it is critical that you identify who your customers are, and what their needs, wants and preferences are. It is also important to discuss what approaches you use in determining your customer requirements, how often you do a "pulse check" of their preferences, and how you include future customers in this determination. One of your first tasks is to correctly identify who your customers are. They are the end-users of your products or services. Without customers, most organizations would cease to exist. For example, if for some reason library patrons cease using libraries, libraries would have to close doors because their function would have become obsolete. That's one of the major reasons why libraries have started to survey customers on their preferences and satisfaction with library services and offerings.

Here is a sampling of the comments of library patrons who participated in a focus group discussion in Delaware.

1. Many participants are pleased with the library service they receive. Their expectations are traditional, namely they are interested in having more books and computers, and others would like to see a greater selection of newspaper collections to include some in foreign languages, specifically Spanish and Russian.

2. Participants are interested in making the library the hub of their communities, providing meeting and gathering spaces for families and people of all ages with programs, exhibits, game nights, and ways to interact with each other.

3. Their descriptions of the perfect library for their community often included meeting spaces for programs and a coffee shop, and separate spaces for noisy activities and quiet activities. They preferred separate spaces for children's story times, young adults, tutoring sessions, and computer terminals. They wanted a dedicated space to view videos and DVDs, and to listen to tapes and CDs at the library.

3.2 Customer Relationships and Satisfaction (45 pts.) Process

Describe HOW your organization builds relationships to acquire, satisfy, and retain CUSTOMERS; to increase CUSTOMER loyalty; and to develop new opportunities. Describe also HOW your organization determines CUSTOMER satisfaction.

What Does This Item Mean?

This Item asks how you satisfy customer demands and how you continue to keep customers happy so they remain loyal. Although it isn't possible to generalize what all customers want in every organization or industry, there are certain change to common attributes that they all want and value, such as convenience, timeliness, low prices, and high quality.

Kano, a notable Japanese quality consultant, proposed an interesting concept on customer requirements, which he divided into three dimensions. They are summarized in Ashok Rao's *Total Quality Management*.

1. "Must-Bes": These are characteristics that customers expect to be present and if they are absent, customers become dissatisfied. These are factors that are taken for granted. For example, when you go to your local library, you expect it to have an ample collection of up-to-date reference books and reading materials. If the books are antiquated and the reference materials are old and obsolete, you will walk out of that library feeling disgruntled and dissatisfied.

2. One-Dimensional: These are characteristics that customers look for and are directly related to customer satisfaction. For example, if the temperature in the library is too hot during a humid summer day, most customers complain and are dissatisfied. As the temperature gets cooler, customer satisfaction increases.

3. Delighters: These are characteristics that excite the customers because they are attractive attributes that are unexpected. They are latent requirements, which customers do not miss if they are not present. For example, when Tespina used the digital library of a local state library, the front desk staff not only assisted her in learning how to access the system and research the topic, but also provided her with additional information and resources (i.e., reference librarian and inter library loan). In addition to being professional, knowledgeable, and courteous, the desk attendant was also friendly and efficient. Tespina came out of the library delighted with the service she had received and vowed she would return to that library the next time she was doing research.

The customer relationships and satisfaction item asks you how you keep customers loyal, returning for repeat business with your agency and telling others about you when you provide them with the expected attributes and delighters. In essence, it asks you to describe the diverse approaches you use to satisfy your different customer groups and how you learn about their requirements.

Focus groups, interviews and surveys are ways of finding out what your customers' preferences and demands are and how satisfied they are with the services your provide. Below is a sampling of customers' perceptions of the positives and negatives of a library system as gleaned from a focus group discussion.

Positives

- Children's programming and services
- The cost savings afforded by the library; patrons don't have to buy the books, videos, and magazines that they borrow from the library
- The ability to place reserves and to renew books online

- Audio book collections, especially unabridged books
- Availability of inter library loan service
- Friendly, helpful staff
- Convenient location,
- Sunday hours

Negatives

- Too many obsolete or old books, especially in nonfiction areas
- The lack of classics in the collections
- Inadequate, outdated music collections
- Noise levels
- Too few computers
- Too few evening hours
- Too little space, including lack of quiet areas and comfortable seating
- Lack of meeting room space
- Too few children's sessions (unable to get in because sessions are filled)
- Lack of services and programs for middle school age children
- Lack of parking
- Lack of handicapped accessibility
- Low staff salaries
- Insufficient numbers of staff
- Online computer catalogs that are hard to use.

Below (Figure 7.2) is a graphical representation of customers' satisfaction with the assistance provided by the staff of the Library for the Blind and the Physically Handicapped (LBPH).

Category 4: Measurement, Analysis and Knowledge Management (90 points)

This category examines the different methods used by organizations in collecting and analyzing data and information to support performance improvements in customer satisfaction, products and services, and business processes. It also looks

---

4.1 Measurement, Analysis, and Review of Organizational Performance (45 pts.) Process

Describe HOW your organization measures, analyzes, aligns, reviews, and improves its PERFORMANCE data and information at all LEVELS and in all parts of your organization.

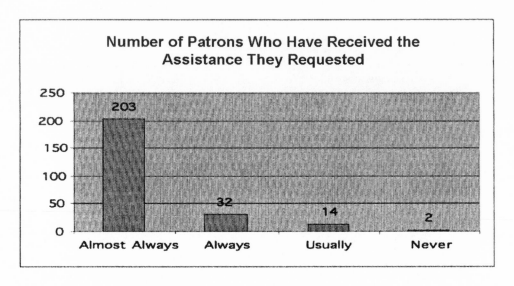

Figure 7.2 *Number of Patrons Who Have Received the Assistance They Requested. Bar Chart Showing LBPH Survey Results, 2005.*

at how organizational knowledge is managed and transmitted throughout the entire organization.

What Does This Item Mean?

This Item asks you to describe what performance metrics you collect and how to measure and to improve the competitive performance of your organization. To achieve and to sustain quality excellence, these metrics are used in decision making (i.e., fact-based) to achieve operational and strategic goals. It must include and balance the differential impact and importance of customers, financial, key organizational processes, and employee and stakeholders' measures using a Balanced Scorecard system as portrayed in Figure 7.3. It is important to include both short-term and long-term metrics that support your mission, your future direction, and your strategies.

It is also important to include both lagging and leading indicators of effectiveness. Leading indicators predict future performance, such as highly skilled and competent employees and efficient processes (leading measures) as key predictors of high customer satisfaction, a lagging measure (see Figure 7.4). If you are delighted with the efficient services provided by competent staff, you are more likely to do repeat business with Library X. Lagging indicators are bottom-line measures resulting from subsequent actions and conditions. For example, employee absenteeism,

Customers

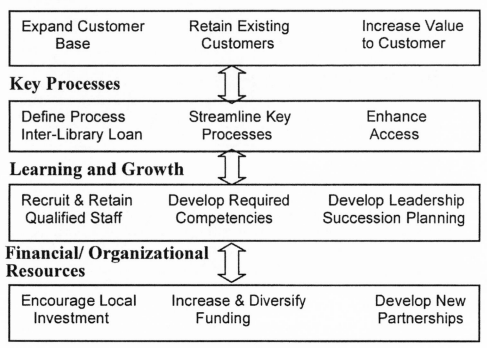

| Expand Customer Base | Retain Existing Customers | Increase Value to Customer |

Key Processes

| Define Process Inter-Library Loan | Streamline Key Processes | Enhance Access |

Learning and Growth

| Recruit & Retain Qualified Staff | Develop Required Competencies | Develop Leadership Succession Planning |

Financial/ Organizational Resources

| Encourage Local Investment | Increase & Diversify Funding | Develop New Partnerships |

Figure 7.3 Sample of a Balanced Metrics in a Library System.

High Customer Satisfaction and Retention

LAGGING MEASURES

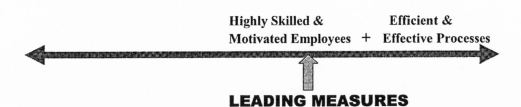

Highly Skilled & Motivated Employees + **Efficient & Effective Processes**

LEADING MEASURES

Figure 7.4 Leading Measures: Predictors of Future Performance and Lagging Measures: Results of Subsequent Actions.

low morale, and low productivity (leading measures) are the precursors and symptoms of poor employee satisfaction, a lagging indicator.

4.2 Information and Knowledge Management (45 pts.) Process

Describe HOW your organization ensures the quality and availability of needed data and information for employees, suppliers and PARTNERS, and CUSTOMERS. Describe HOW your organization builds and manages its KNOWLEDGE ASSETS.

What Does This Item Mean?

This Item asks you how you communicate data to your employees, partners and customers. The first step is to make sure that you are sharing data and metrics that are simple, accurate, and relate to important services, activities and products that are Critical-To-Quality (CTQ) factors. Although there is a strong temptation to measure everything, since we have been programmed to do so by mandated federal reports, we have to resist that urge. It is not a federal offense to design and collect 15 to 20 metrics that are simple, easy to collect, easy to understand, and relevant to your business outcomes. Your metrics must provide prompt feedback to users so that corrections and adjustments can be done relatively quickly. Managers and employees need real-time performance reports that do not take a year or two to prepare so they can correct problems immediately. A division we worked with shared information with users by prominently displaying dashboard measures results in a bulletin board in the office corridors. In addition, the metrics were also visually portrayed in graphs, charts, and diagrams in the Intranet, in monthly newsletters, and in weekly reports sent to staff and the cabinet secretary. This communication system provides all users easy and efficient access to available information. This Item also asks how you ensure that hardware and software are reliable and user-friendly. A state library ensured data quality and usability by taking the following steps, which were outlined in its Baldrige Quality Award application.

> *Library XYZ relies on three key components to ensure the reliability of hardware and software: 1) Reliable technology by using only reputable suppliers; 2) competent IT staff who keep their knowledge and skills current with new technology; and 3) sound IT management practices by complying with state technology policies and mandates.*
>
> *There are several levels of protection to ensure security and confidentiality of data. All employees have a user ID and highly secure passwords to access the data and information on their PCs. Programmatically, the passwords are forced to be changed regularly. The network itself is protected by a variety of security devises like firewalls and virus protection software. Security is also*

strengthened through the Department of Technology and Information (DTI) Policy and Procedures manual. Every state employee is mandated to sign and comply with the Internet and PC Acceptable Use Policy.

In the event of an emergency, Library XYZ ensures the continued availability of data and information by providing backups for data and power for all critical servers and the data that they contain. Data backups are conducted in full on a daily basis. All personal computers are protected by battery backups and virus protection software that are constantly updated. All PCs are reimaged on a regular basis with industry standard software to ensure system integrity.

Finally, this Item asks how you transmit organizational knowledge to your employees, managers, councils, board members, and other stakeholders. Do you have cross training, mentoring, coaching, or a formalized leadership-employee training program? Do you document key business processes and procedures in a policy and procedures manual, or capture information in a shared drive on your agency's intranet? You can employ any methods to share organizational learnings, as long as they provide easy and efficient access to those who need to use them.

Category 5: Human Resource Focus (85 points)

This category looks at how an agency enables employees to realize their full potential as they pursue the organization's quality objectives and performance goals.

5.1 Work Systems (35 pts.)

Describe HOW your organization's work and jobs enable employees and the organization to achieve HIGH PERFORMANCE. Describe HOW compensation, career progression, and related workforce practices enable employees and the organization to achieve HIGH PERFORMANCE.

What Does This Item Mean?

In this Item you are asked to address how you and your organization achieve the goal of high performance in the ways your work and jobs are designed. For example, your work units might be organized as self-directed teams, cross-functional teams, process teams, divisions, or departments. Do these work structures facilitate or impede efficiency, agility, and productivity? You are also asked to provide evidence as to how your HR system — the way you select, develop, retain, and reward employees — contributes to high performance. For example, you might select and hire employees using Competency-Based Interviewing (CBI). CBI is an interviewing process that is focused on getting the individual to recount a layered story of past events that provide evidence of the presence or absence of a competency. Competencies are patterns of behavior that distinguish high performers from others in the same job classification. The state of Maine selected ten core leadership competencies that form the basis of the questions asked of all new hires applying for the managerial and leadership track. The logic behind this method of interviewing is that "past behavior is the best predictor of future success." The purpose of CBI is to look for clear evidence that the applicant has demonstrable experience in performing the desired competencies because he or she has done them in the past. For example, if an individual has demontrated strong leadership skills in his or her past jobs, he or she is more likely to succeed in the present job that requires comparable skills and abilities.

You are also asked if you considered cultural factors in the design of your jobs and your organizational structures. As we all know, the world of work has changed significantly. There are more women and minorities in the workforce now than any time in history. The U.S. Bureau of Labor Statistics: 1996–2006 study projected that the percent change for women (+14.2 percent), Asians (+41.0 percent), and Hispanics (+36.2 percent) in the workforce will be monumental. Given the fact that the workforce demographics have changed, have you as an organization made adjustments in designing your work functions and structures? For example, the management of a non-profit agency in a northeastern state, where a majority of workers are women, implemented flexible work schedules, dual-incumbencies or job-sharing arrangements, and started a small day care center.

5.2 Employee Learning and Motivation (25 pts.)

Describe HOW your organization's employee education, training, and career development support the achievement of your overall objectives and contribute to HIGH PERFORMANCE. Describe HOW your organization's education, training, and career development build employee knowledge, skills, and capabilities.

What Does This Item Mean?

In this Item, you are asked how your employee training and development support the achievement of your organization's strategic objectives and how they enhance employees' skills, knowledge, and abilities. In other words, your training plan and strategy have to flow out and be inextricably linked to your overall organizational strategic plan and objectives. Individual learning plans should be linked not only to individual employee needs but also to organizational needs and priorities. It is therefore important to do a training needs analysis before spending thousands of dollars on training that is not needed.

Statistics released by the American Association of Training and Development noted that employers spend approximately 50 to 60 billion dollars on employee training. Given the enormous investment in time and money, it only makes sense to first figure out if training is needed and whether it is the right solution to a performance problem.

Below is a sample training needs analysis model (Figure 7.5). It shows the importance of conducting a training needs analysis at the organization, person and task analyses levels. Organizations typically start by looking at organizational priorities and then move on to analyzing task and individual employee needs. It is also important to remember that not all performance problems can be successfully solved by training. For example, a fiscal unit in a state library setting has a vendor pay-

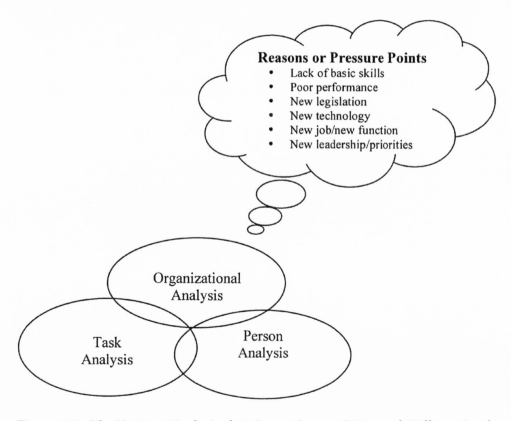

Figure 7.5 *The Training Needs Analysis Process Pressure Points and Different Levels.* *Source: Adapted from Raymond Noe,* Employee Training and Development *(1998).*

ment backlog of six months and for the last two years has been unable to pay bills in a timely fashion. Some of the reasons for the fiscal problem include the inability of the new fiscal officer to lead, the staff's lack of motivation and teamwork, a culture of distrust and favoritism, and the use of obsolete technology. The first two reasons or "pressure points" for late payments could be addressed by training, but the last two require other interventions.

In addition to providing training that is useful to the organization and to the employees, implicit in the Item is the need to find out if the training intervention is effective or not. You have to provide evidence that the training resulted in an improvement in knowledge, skills, capabilities, and behavior. A good model to use in evaluating training effectiveness is the classic model introduced by Donald L. Kirkpatrick (1994), which is outlined in Table 7.1.

The data for the reaction and learning levels are collected before employees return to their jobs. The data for the behavioral and results levels are collected when employees return to work and are designed to measure the transfer of learning to on-the-job behaviors. In summary, this Item looks both at how you identify training needs of the organization and individual employees, and how the learning and competencies are transferred and used to do jobs.

<table>
<tr><td colspan="3">Table 7.1
Kirkpatrick's Four-Level Training Evaluation</td></tr>
<tr><td>Levels</td><td>Criteria</td><td>Focus and Examples</td></tr>
<tr><td>1</td><td>Reaction</td><td>Trainee satisfaction. Examples: Survey of trainee's satisfaction with instructor, topic, handouts, facility, visual aids/technology, and food.</td></tr>
<tr><td>2</td><td>Learning</td><td>Acquisition of cognitive skills, knowledge, capabilities and desired attitudes. Examples: Pretest and posttest of topic learned; work sample.</td></tr>
<tr><td>3</td><td>Behavior</td><td>Improvement and change of behavior on the job. Examples: Observation and interviews by subject matter experts; work sample; rating by peers and supervisors; and job description review.</td></tr>
<tr><td>4</td><td>Results</td><td>Positive outcomes for the organization. Examples: Return on investment; increase in productivity; reduction of accidents; reduction in turnover; and increased customer satisfaction.</td></tr>
</table>

Figure 7.1 Kirkpatrick's Four-Level Training Program.

5.3 Employee Well-Being and Satisfaction (25 pts.)

Process

Describe HOW your organization maintains a work environment and an employee support climate that contribute to the well-being, satisfaction, and motivation of all employees.

What Does This Item Mean?

The central theme of the Baldrige approach is the focus on customer satisfaction, which is impossible to achieve without first satisfying your internal customers, your employees. In this Item, you are asked how you take preventive measures to ensure the safety, health, security and ergonomic accommodation of your employees. It also asks what proactive plans you have in place to protect your employees from disasters and other emergency situations, to ensure that they are safe, and that business continues smoothly. This question was added after the terrorist attack of September 11, 2001, and it assumed greater significance with hurricanes Katrina, Rita, and Wilma in 2005.

Similar to the customer requirements asked about in Category 3, this Item also addresses how you determine the requirements of your employees that affect their satisfaction and well-being. You are also asked to segment preferences based on the demographic and cultural diversity of your workforce and their functional responsibilities.

Finally, you are asked to address how you measure your employees' satisfaction index and what measurement indicators are used to assess their job satisfaction. Here, it is important to use both soft (i.e., employee morale and motivation) and hard (i.e., absenteeism, retention, and grievances) measures of satisfaction and to include both formal (i.e., surveys, questionnaires, and interviews) and informal (i.e., managing by walking and talking) methods. A popular and admired leader from one of the agencies we worked with spent a portion of his workday walking around and getting to know all 450 employees and calling them by their first names. He also rewarded the employees of the month by taking them out to lunch or breakfast, and paying for their meals out of his own pocket. It does not matter if the methods employed are formal or informal as long as they are systematic, predictable, consistent, and effective.

Category 6: Process Management (85 points)

This category focuses on the use of systematic approaches in the design, management and improvement of value-creation (i.e., key business processes) and support processes.

> **6.1 Value Creation Processes (45 pts.)**
>
> Describe HOW your organization identifies and manages its KEY PROCESSES for creating CUSTOMER VALUE and achieving business success and growth.

What Does This Item Mean?

No matter how knowledgeable, well trained and capable your employees are, their motivation will suffer if they have to work with ineffective and inefficient processes. How many times have you heard employees complain about work processes that don't make sense, are repetitive, and do not add value to the outcome? In our experience as quality consultants, we've heard disgruntled and dispirited employees whisper, "Do we need 33 steps to assess eligibility and why do we even need authorization from our boss before we can declare client X eligible for the service?" "Why do we need to have five sign offs before we can pay a bill?" All these are obsolete control and inspection systems that impede the achievement of agency goals and destroy employee motivation and creativity. This Item asks you how you manage and improve your key work processes to satisfy customers, including your employees, and how you improve overall agency performance.

Some examples of systematic approaches to improving processes are the use of the PDSA method, flow-charting and process reengineering. Mike Hammer and James Champy wrote *Reengineering the Corporation* (1993), the seminal book on the concept of reengineering, which they defined as using "the power of information technology to radically redesign our business processes in order to achieve dramatic improvements in their performance." Reengineering management gained popularity when James Champy wrote the book on the subject in 1995. Reengineering is a dramatic departure from the old ways of changing work processes because it seeks to implement quantum improvements by focusing on the redesign of core business processes, not non-critical ones. Champy advised against the application of incremental change. Instead he encouraged management to mobilize employees to team up with leaders in making deep and fundamental changes in their core work processes. It assumes that the existing process is not working, so it encourages organizations to start out with a clean slate by "wiping out" the poorly designed process and replacing it with a new one. He noted that "the larger the scale of change, the greater the opportunity for success" (*Reengineering Management*, "Questions that Readers Ask Most"). Below is a visual representation of the steps in process reengineering, using Champy's ideas as a model.

This Item also asks you to identify your key work processes and their key requirements, measures, and improvement strategies. Below is an example from the

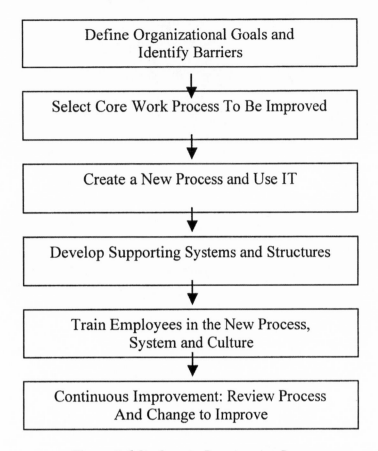

Figure 7.6 *Six Steps in Reengineering Process.*

DDL application showing the response to Item 6.1 in Category 6 on "Key Value Creation Processes" (i.e., key work processes) and their "Key Requirements."

Table 7.2 Sample Key Value Creation Process and Key Requirements	
Key Value Creation Process	*Key Performance Requirement*
Statewide Library Planning and Development	• Improve libraries (national rankings) by identifying and resolving problems with previous years' planning and library service processes • Meet customer, supplier, staff, and stakeholder needs and preferences

Table 7.2
Sample Key Value Creation Process
and Key Requirements

Key Value Creation Process	Key Performance Requirement
State and Federal Funding	• Have a balanced budget in support of key functions, programs, and priorities • Complete annual budget in promptly • Make efficient and accurate day-to-day financial transactions • Maintain integrity of financial and reporting systems
Collection Development	• Ensure collections meet customer demands
Professional Development	• Hold stakeholder, partner, and staff training to support quality and high-level library services
Delaware Center for the Book	• BookProvide targeted programming and lifelong learning opportunities to meet customer needs and preferences
Reference	• Focus on adequate and quality collection (i.e., books and other forms of information) • Provide state-of-the-art technology • Give library staff training for providing reference services and quality customer service

---

6.2 Support Processes (40 pts.)

Describe HOW your organization manages its KEY PROCESSES that support your VALUE CREATION PROCESSES. Describe your PROCESSES for financial management and continuity of operations in an emergency.

What Does This Item Mean?

This Item is similar to Item 6.1 on value creation processes and asks comparable questions except that it focuses on your organization's support processes. Support processes include activities that are carried out by the organization in support of core work processes to achieve its primary mission and vision. A sample response to support processes and key process requirements from a governmental agency follows.

**Table 7.3
Sample Support Processes
and Key Requirements**

Support Processes	*Process Requirements*
1. Financial	• Balanced budget • Diversification of funding source • No material findings on federal and state audits • Compliance with state and federal requirements
2. Information Technology	• Computer data accuracy and integrity • State-of-the art technology • Daily back-up of operational systems to enhance system up-time • Compliance with the state's Computer System Acceptable Use Policy • Compliance with federal requirements for computer-generated data
3. Human Resource	• Alignment of training intervention with employee and organizational needs • Provision of continuing & effective training • High employee satisfaction • Ensure health, safety and security of employees • High employee satisfaction with benefits, work-load, job design and work environment • Provide accommodations for employees with dis-abilities • Use of Competency-Based Interview method in the selection process and use of exit interview to enhance retention
4. Facilities Management	• Provide safe, clean and well-designed facilities and offices • Ensure prompt response and effective resolution of facility-related problems
5. Communication	• Provide up-to-date and accurate information on key data/information, major activities, and key changes to all employees • Develop communication plan for key initiatives, such as a quality project: identify strategies, accountabilities, rewards and training • Use different media to share two-way communications

Category 7: Business Results (450 points)

The results section refers to the ways in which an organization's effectiveness and improvement trends are reflected in performance outcomes and performance levels relative to those of their competitors. This is a major category and ranks as the highest scoring category — 450 points out of a total of 1000 points. There should be consistency and alignment with the data and information you present in items 1.1, 3.2, 4.1, 5.0, and 6.0 because they all refer to performance measures.

There are certain practices and recommendations you should be aware of when you present data and statistics in Category 7. Here are some general pointers for the use of graphics and charts to portray your organization's business results.

- Use comparison measures and benchmarks.
- Use statistics for a three- to five-year historical period to display trends and patterns of improvement and growth.
- Bar graphs or charts should show a positive trend. If there is a trend variation or decline, explain to the reader the reasons for such deviations and discuss what you are doing to correct them.
- Display all your results in graphical forms, with a short narrative explaining the emerging trend or pattern.
- Display data in simple graphical formats such as bar charts, histograms, pie charts, and scattergrams, to name a few. When you graph numerical information, you get a better sense of the meaning of the data presented.
- Avoid portraying complex data and multiple measures in a single graph. The purpose of the visual representation is to make the data understandable and meaningful, not confusing.
- Make sure the data and the data points presented in a graphical format are large enough to be readable. Packing information in a single graph does nothing to enhance understanding.
- Use color graphs and charts to make clear distinctions and comparisons between performance periods, segmentation of customers, process variations, and other comparison measures.
- In general, use the most recent historical data to display performance, preferably in annual increments. Yearly comparisons have more statistical power in terms of validity and reliability because they represent sustained periods of performance.
- Establish baseline data to make meaningful comparisons. When observing changes in behavior, such as transfer of learning to on-the-job tasks, it is critical to establish baseline data of the behavior before the "treatment" (i.e., train-

ing) was applied. Baseline data allow for appropriate adaptation periods to occur and for any unusual changes in the environment, such as a subject matter expert or a supervisor watching the employee apply the new skill learned during training. Using a pretest to gather baseline data to assess if learning has occurred allows for a meaningful comparison with posttest data.

- In general, large samples are preferable to small samples because they are less prone to sampling errors, are more reliable, and have greater statistical power.

7.1 Product and Service Outcomes (100 pts.) Results

Summarize your organization's KEY product and service PERFORMANCE RESULTS. SEGMENT your RESULTS by product and service types and groups, CUSTOMER groups, and market SEGMENTS, as appropriate. Include appropriate comparative data.

What Does This Item Mean?

This first Item asks for performance data related to customer requirements and expectations, such as cycle time or timeliness, efficiency and accuracy. This is an important section because it is related to the fundamental purpose of the organization — its mission.

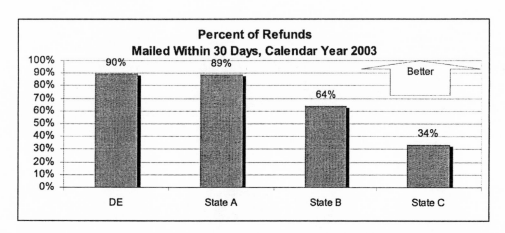

Figure 7.7 *Percent of Refunds Mailed Within 30 Days, Calendar Year 2003. Bar Chart Comparing Delaware's Cycle Time to Other States*

Notice that Figure 7.7 displays not only the statistics for the applicant's refund cycle time but also comparison measures from other states performing similar func-

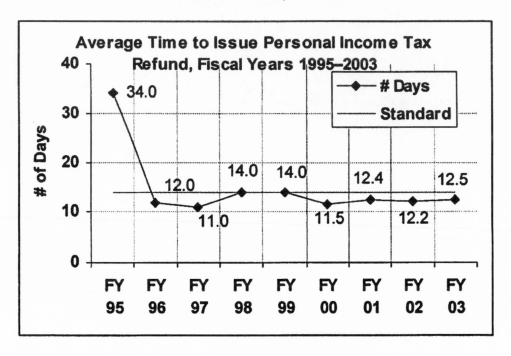

Figure 7.8 Average Time to Issue Personal Income Tax Refund, Fiscal Years 1995–2003. Graph Comparing Personal Income Tax Refund Cycle Time.

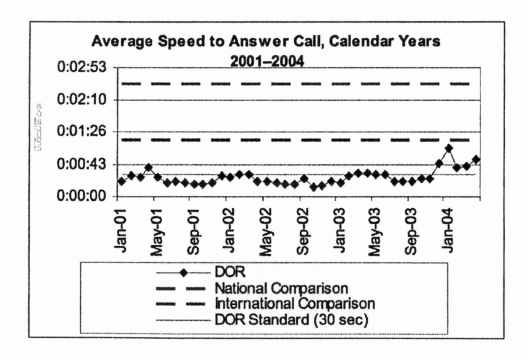

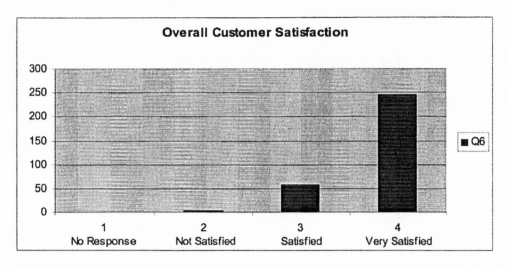

Figure 7.10 *Overall Customer Satisfaction. Bar Chart Showing Overall Customer Satisfaction.*

tions. Comparisons with three states with processes similar to "applicant DE" suggest that their current performance level is highly competitive.

Figure 7.8 shows the improvement trend in the agency's performance from 1995 through 2003. Although the improvement was not sustained for the entire nine-year period, the emerging trend for all the historical data presented demonstrated a decrease in the number of days it takes to issue a personal income tax (PIT) refund and a clear compliance with standard norms, with the exception of the baseline year, 1995.

Note in Figure 7.9 that "applicant DOR's" standard and performance exceed both national and international benchmarks.

7.2 Customer-Focused Results (70 pts.)

Summarize your organization's KEY CUSTOMER-focused RESULTS, including CUSTOMER satisfaction and CUSTOMER perceived VALUE. SEGMENT your RESULTS by product and service types and groups, CUSTOMER groups, and market SEGMENTS as appropriate. Include appropriate comparative data.

What Does This Item Mean?

This Item asks for performance data related to customer satisfaction and dissatisfaction. You are also asked to include performance data on customer loyalty, reten-

Opposite: Figure 7.9 *Average Speed to Answer Calls, Calendar Years 2001–2004. Line Graph Depicting Average Speed to Answer Calls.*

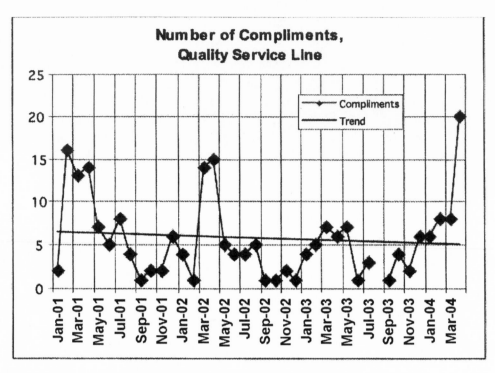

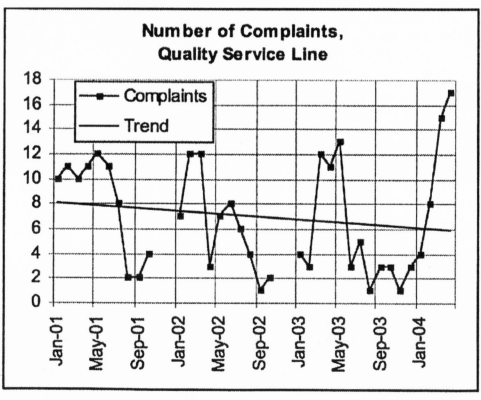

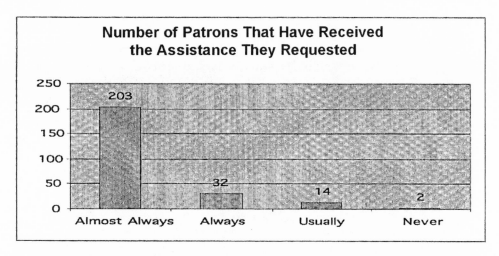

Figure 7.13 *Number of Patrons That Have Received the Assistance They Requested. Assistance Received from the Library for the Blind and Physically Handicapped, Calendar Year 2005.*

tion, positive referrals and other aspects related to building relationships with customers. Finally, you are asked to segment your customer results and present comparison data. Figure 7.10 shows the overall customer satisfaction of an organization, which is a key determinant of organizational effectiveness. Assessing organizational performance without this critical measure would yield an incomplete scorecard, at best.

Compliment and complaint levels are shown on Figures 7.11 and 7.12. The upward trends, especially the rising number of complaints during the months of March, April and May, need to be explained in the narrative. You also need to address what steps are being taken to alleviate this emerging problem.

Figure 7.13 shows the level of satisfaction with the services received by individuals with disabilities, demonstrating that the applicant is aware of the need to display data on diverse customer groups.

7.3 Financial and Market Results (70 pts.)
Summarize your organization's KEY financial and marketplace PERFORMANCE RESULTS by CUSTOMER or market SEGMENTS, as appropriate. Include appropriate comparative data.

Opposite, top: **Figure 7.11** *Number of Compliments, Quality Service Line. Number of Compliments, Quality Service Line Quarterly Comparison 2001–2004.* **Bottom: Figure 7.12** *Number of Complaints, Quality Service Line. Number of Complaints, Quality Service Line Quarterly Comparison 2001–2004.*

What Does This Item Mean?

This Item asks for two types of performance data — market and financial results. Financial measures might include revenues, return on investment, absence of material audit findings, and diversification of revenue sources. Market measures might include new services and products, increase in per capita library visits, circulation and reference transactions. Sample responses gleaned from actual applications are presented in Figures 7.14, 7.15, 7.16 and 7.17.

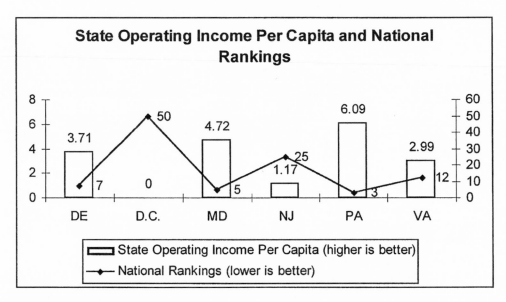

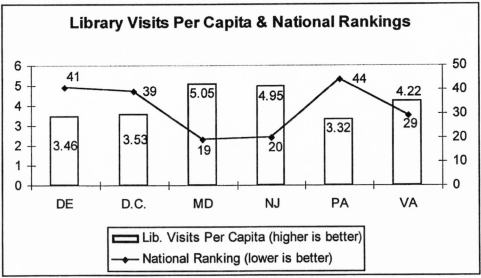

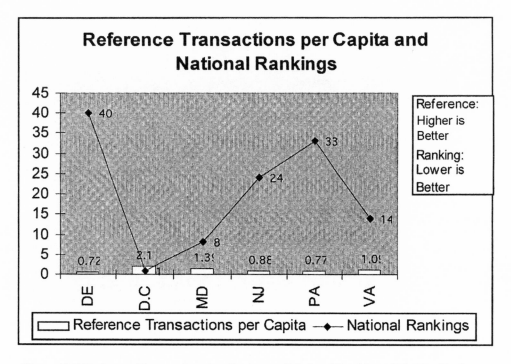

Figure 7.16 *Reference Transactions Per Capita and National Rankings. Relationship between Reference Transactions Per Capita and National Library Rankings.*

7.4 Human Resource Results (70 pts.)
Summarize your organization's KEY human resource RESULTS, including WORK SYSTEM PERFORMANCE and employee LEARNING, development, well-being, and satisfaction. SEGMENT your RESULTS to address the DIVERSITY of your workforce and the different types and categories of employees, as appropriate. Include appropriate comparative data.

What Does This Item Mean?

This Item asks for performance data related to the effectiveness of the agency's work systems, levels of employee satisfaction, and the quality of the employee training and development. Figures 7.18 and 7.19 are sample responses from actual applications from a library agency and a state agency.

A majority of the staff from the applicant organization has been with the organ-

Opposite, top: Figure 7.14 *State Operating Income Per Capita and National Rankings. Relationship between Library Visits Per Capita and National Library Rankings.*

Bottom: Figure 7.15 *Library Visits Per Capita and National Rankings. Relationship between Library Visits Per Capita and National Library Rankings.*

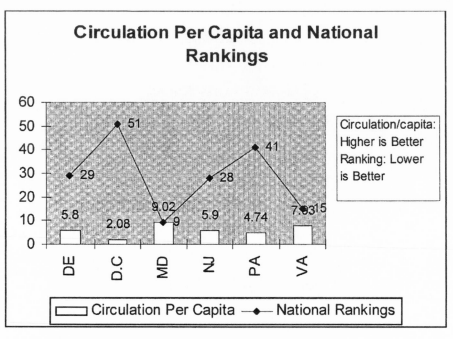

Circulation Per Capita and National Rankings

Circulation/capita: Higher is Better
Ranking: Lower is Better

Legend: ☐ Circulation Per Capita ◆ National Rankings

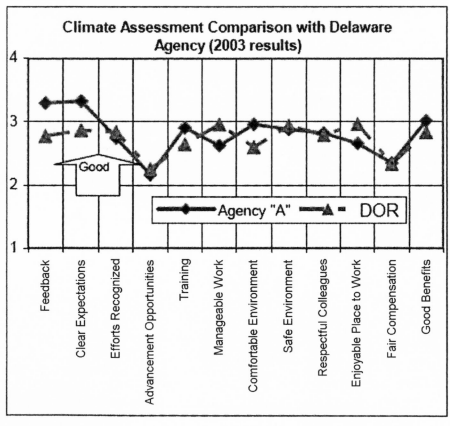

Climate Assessment Comparison with Delaware Agency (2003 results)

Legend: ◆ Agency "A" ▲ DOR

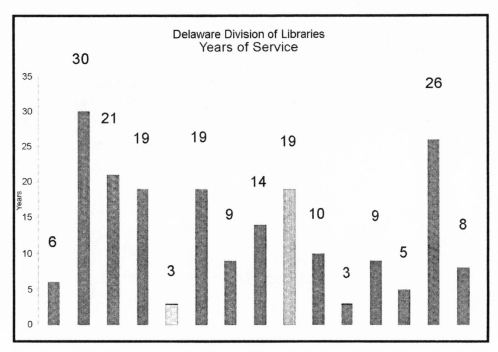

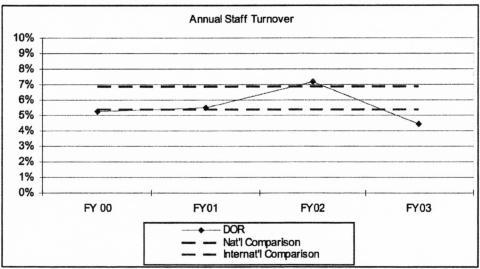

Opposite, top: Figure 7.17 Ciculation Per Capita and National Rankings. Relationship between Circulation Per Capita and National Library Rankings.

Bottom: Figure 7.18 Climate Assessment Comparison with Top Delaware Agency. Climate Assessment for Applicant Agency Comparison with Top Performing Agency, Calendar Year 2003.

Above, top: Figure 7.19 Delaware Division of Libraries Years of Service. Staff Retention, in Years. *Bottom: Figure 7.20* Annual Staff Turnover. Percent of Annual Staff Turnover, Fiscal Years 2000–2003.

105

ization for ten years or more, which indicates high employee retention, a direct measure of employee well-being and satisfaction.

Figures 7.20 and 7.21 relate to employee separations and promotions. The number of separations is compared with national and international benchmarks. Although the number of promotions available is limited, the majority of promotions were filled by employees working for the applicant organization.

7.5 Organizational Effectiveness Results (70 pts.)

Summarize your organization's KEY operational PERFORMANCE RESULTS that contribute to the improvement of organizational effectiveness. SEGMENT your RESULTS by product and service types and groups and by market SEGMENTS, as appropriate. Include appropriate comparative data.

What Does This Item Mean?

In this Item, you are asked to present performance data on the effectiveness of both your key business and support processes. Typical measures might include cycle time, flexibility, accuracy, productivity, use of e-technology, innovation rates, and other strategies employed to maximize process efficiency and accuracy (e.g., Six Sigma and process reengineering initiatives). You are also asked to segment your results by service and product types and by market segments (i.e., program offerings for different customer groups). Figures 7.22 and 7.23 (both are sample applications) show the increasing number of personal income tax returns filed using e-technology and that the applicant agency exceeded national standards in the area under consideration.

7.6 Leadership and Social Responsibility Results (70 pts.)

Summarize your organization's KEY GOVERNANCE, SENIOR LEADERSHIP, and social responsibility RESULTS, including evidence of ETHICAL BEHAVIOR, fiscal accountability, legal compliance, and organizational citizenship. SEGMENT your RESULTS by business units, as appropriate. Include appropriate comparative data.

What Does This Item Mean?

In this final Item, you are asked to summarize your key performance results demonstrating ethical and socially responsible behavior, compliance with legal and statutory requirements, fiscal responsibility, and achievement of strategic goals and

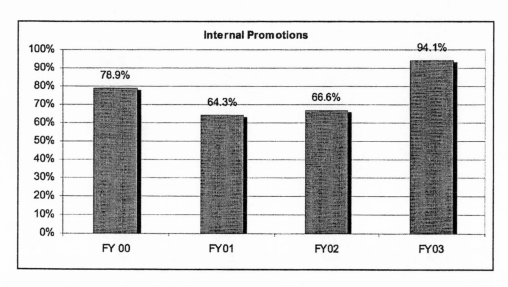

Figure 7.21 *Internal Promotions. Percent of Internal Promotions, Fiscal Years 2000–2003.*

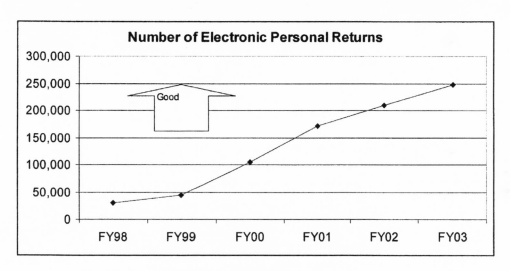

Figure 7.22 *Number of Electronic Personal Returns. Number of Personal Income Tax Returns Filed Using E-Technology, Fiscal Years 1998–2003.*

action plans. Measures of results might include the number of dismissals or disciplinary actions due to unethical behavior, the number of employees completing ethics training, and the number of citations or sanctions for legal or regulatory violations. Measures of fiscal accountability might include audit findings, reduction of deficit, increased level of financial oversight and review, and reduction in the disparity between senior leaders and employees' pay. Measures of good citizenship and support of key communities might include support of charitable and other community organizations through voluntary activities and financial contributions.

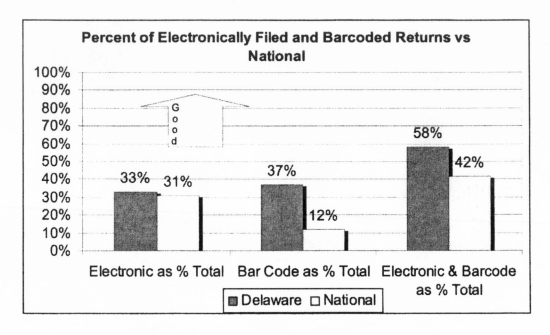

Figure 7.23 *Percent of Electronically Filed and Barcoded Returns vs. National. Use of E-Technology and "Bar Coding" to Facilitate Customer Income Tax Filing.*

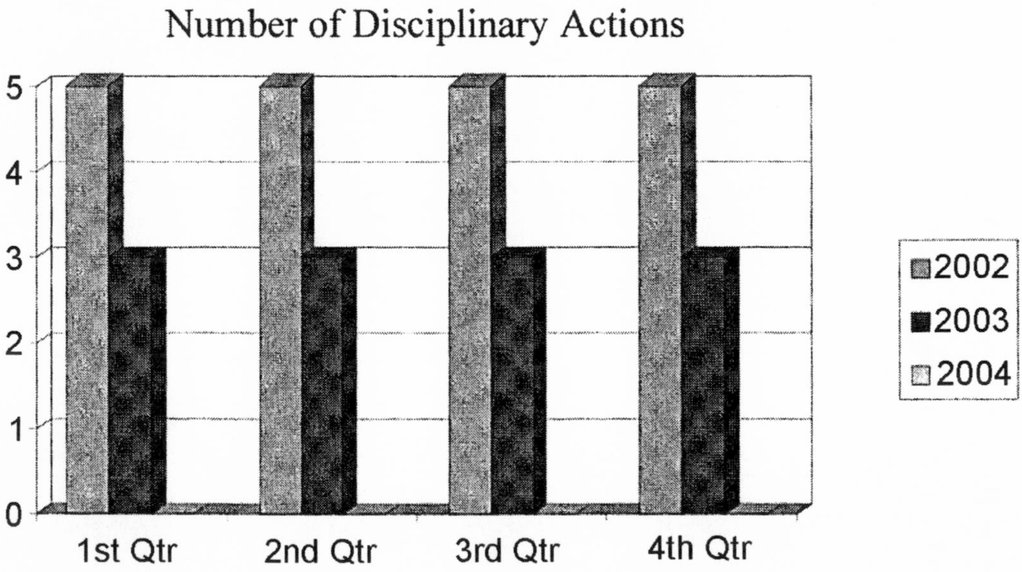

Number of Disciplinary Actions

Figure 7.24 *Number of Disciplinary Actions. Number of Disciplinary Actions Due to Violations of Ethical or Moral Conduct for XYZ Library, 2002–2004.*

As shown in Figure 7.24, for calendar year 2004, there was not a single recorded case reflecting violations of ethical or moral conduct brought before the Council on Libraries or the State Public Integrity Commission for XYZ Library, a "fictitious" library. This figure represents a significant decrease in the number of violations recorded in 2003 and 2004, when compared with 2002.

8

Application Template of the Baldrige Criteria

"Learning is not compulsory ... neither is survival."
— Dr. W. Edwards
Deming (1900–1993)

A template of the Baldrige Quality organizational profile, categories, Items and areas to address and how they apply to libraries is presented below as a useful guide for starting the quality journey. Only selected Items and areas to address are presented in the table below.

Baldrige Quality Award Application and Sample Response from a Library Applicant

ORGANIZATIONAL PROFILE

The organizational profile is a snapshot of your organization, the key influences on how you operate, and the key challenges you face.

P.1a (2) What is your organizational culture? What are your stated purpose, vision, mission, and values?

RRESPONSE FROM A SAMPLE LIBRARY APPLICATION

P.1 a (2) Culture: DDL is a learning organization with a flat organizational structure, which encourages professional development (Figure 5.1–1), two-way communication (Fig. 1.1–2) and the opportunity for active participation of all employees in decision-making through the Plan-Do-Study-Act process (Fig. 6.1–4).

Vision
Providing Delawareans the best libraries in the nation
Every Delawarean will have a library card, and will use it often!

Mission

To provide leadership and support for the timely development of Delaware's libraries to ensure convenient access to and encourage use of current information resources and reading material by all Delawareans.

Values

Service, Access, and Excellence

CATEGORY 1—LEADERSHIP (120 POINTS)

The Leadership Category examines how your organization's senior leaders address values, directions, and performance expectations, as well as a focus on customers and other stakeholders, empowerment, innovation, and learning. Also examined are your organizations, governance and how your organization addresses its public and community responsibilities.

1.2 Governance and Social Responsibility (50 Points)
1.2b (2) Ethical Behavior

How does your organization promote and ensure ethical behavior in all your interactions? What are your key processes and measures or indicators for enabling and monitoring ethical behavior in your governance structure, throughout your organization, and in interactions with customers and partners? How do you monitor and respond to breaches of ethical behavior?

1.2b (1) & (2) Senior DDL leaders are held accountable to the library community and all its _serves at the pleasure of the secretary of state, and can be removed if management accountability is not met, or operations are not carried out in an ethical manner. DDL is closely guided by all financial policies, checks and balances, guidelines and processes of the Auditors Office and State Budget and Accounting Office in relation to the use and handling of state, federal, capital, and other funds. DDL follows state purchasing guidelines which ensure that contracts are awarded through a request for proposal, and committee selections by individual ranking.

The Attorney General's Office provided DDL with a "boiler-plate" contract which includes all important legal aspects to protect the interests of DDL and the State of Delaware and ensures vendor services are rendered in a legal and timely manner. All contracts are internally reviewed by the director, the project manager, and the management analyst.

Selection of personnel is governed by the State Personnel Office guidelines and is conducted through group interviews using questions approved by the State Personnel Office. There are processes in place throughout all public libraries that protect children from being exposed to unethical and inappropriate information and material on the Internet. There are also ethical Internet use guidelines for adult library users. When a violation of the Internet Use Policy occurs, legal authorities are notified and a statewide e-mail is initiated by the "victim" library to all public library directors making them aware of the person's name, circumstance and estimated release date from legal authorities. Through this process, libraries are cautioned about not allowing this person to use the library services for the time period imposed by the legal authorities. Patron confidentiality is protected under the Delaware Code.

The Council on Libraries is advisory and is covered under the Public Integrity Commission. Appointments are balanced politically between the governor and the three counties. Members of the Delaware Library Association adhere to the American Library Association Bill of Rights. In the event of documented verifiable unethical behavior, employees are disciplined or terminated commensurate with the severity of the offense and in accordance with the State Merit Rules.

All of the stakeholders uphold the American Library Association's Library Bill of Rights and uphold the privacy of library records.

CATEGORY 2—STRATEGIC PLANNING (85 POINTS)

The **Strategic Planning Category** examines how your organization develops strategic objectives and action plans. Also examined are how your chosen strategic objectives and action plans are

2.1 Strategy Development (40 Points)

(1) **What are your key strategic objectives and your timetable for accomplishing them? What are your most important goals for these strategic objectives?**

RESPONSE FROM A SAMPLE LIBRARY APPLICATION

2.1b (1) Strategic Objectives

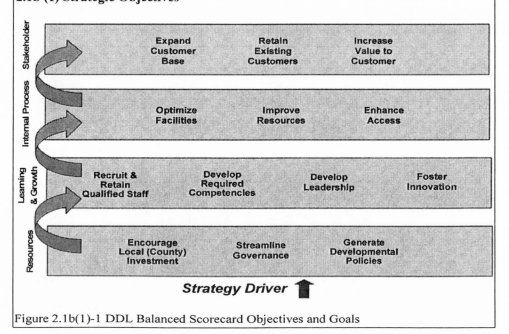

Figure 2.1b(1)-1 DDL Balanced Scorecard Objectives and Goals

CATEGORY 3—CUSTOMER AND MARKET FOCUS (85 POINTS)

The **Customer and Market Focus Category** examines how your organization determines requirements, expectations and preferences of customers and markets. Also examined is how your organization builds relationships with customers and determines key factors that lead to customer acquisition, satisfaction, loyalty and retention, and business expansion.

3.1a (3) How do you keep your listening and learning methods current with business needs and directions, including changes in your marketplace?

3.2b (4) How do you keep your approaches to building relationships and providing customer access current with business needs and directions?

RESPONSE FROM A SAMPLE LIBRARY APPLICATION

3.1a (3)

The division keeps listening and learning methods current with the needs of its customers and the changes in the external environment by implementing the strategies outlined below:

Segment	Listening/Learning Method	Frequency
Public Libraries and the Library Community in Stakeholders.	• Town Meetings	BA
	• Surveys	A, AH
	• Research	A, AH
	• Focus Groups	A, AH
	• Automation Services meetings	A, AH M
	• Technology (Some examples — Intergrated Library System; Virtual Reference)	D M, D, A, BA A
	• Statewide Master Plan	A
	• Communication Methods (Fig. 1.1-2)	A, BA, D, M, Q, W

Figure 3.1-3 Types of Listening and Learning Methods (A=annually, AH=ad hoc, BA=bi-annually, D=daily, M=monthly, Q=quarterly, W=weekly

Additionally, DDL continuously monitors societal trends that affect our services and customers (Figures 2.1–3 and 2.1–4 environmental scans). We keep our listening and learning methods current by learning about and utilizing user-friendly and affordable technologies and facilitation techniques by applying the Plan-Do-Study-Act method (Fig. 6.1–4).

To elaborate on Figure 3.1–3, some of the listening and learning method results include the following:

- OBE (Outcome-Based Evaluation) surveys of end users related to performing arts series led to Best Practices for Programming Kit (available upon request).
- Information obtained from training surveys resulted in more effective training and class offerings that are relevant to job duties, as evidenced by full enrollment in classes. (See figure in section 7.5).
- Biennial survey of LBPH customers resulted in improved collection development (See figure in section 7.1).
- Evaluation surveys after biannual Library Town Meetings resulted in more customer-focused topics on future

Town Meetings (See satisfaction rate results in section 7.2)

The training evaluations determine the appropriateness and timeliness of topics, subject matter relevance to staff's training needs, instructor competencies and other environmental factors. The findings of the surveys are used to drive improvements for the next training intervention.

Question

3.2b (4) How do you keep your approaches to building relationships and providing customer access current with business needs and directions?

Response

3.2b (4) DDL employs the following approaches to keep customer satisfaction methods current with business needs and directions:

- DDL staff gathers data and statistics about individual programs and report the information to the state librarian. The state librarian and DDL staff analyze data collected, identify trends and key findings. Suggestions for improvement are made and implemented based on the key findings. Customer feedback is used to improve and refine programs and services. For example, the Summer Library Reading Program customer survey statistics are collected and analyzed to ensure that program remains effective and responsive to the needs and requirements of its customers. Training evaluations are collected and analyzed to ensure that courses are appropriate to customer needs.
- The LBPH partners with the Consumer Advisory Council in supporting the agency's budget, in strategic planning efforts, and in identifying new program services and emerging needs. The program's customer satisfaction survey is reviewed annually to reflect the ever-changing needs of its customer base.
- SWOT (Strengths, Weaknesses, Opportunities and Threats) analysis (Figures 2.1–3 and 4)
- PDSA process (Figure 6.1–4)
- Listening and Learning methods (Figure 3.1–3)
- Customer Relationships (Figure 3.1–4)

CATEGORY 4—MEASUREMENT, ANALYSIS, AND
KNOWLEDGE MANAGEMENT (90 POINTS)

The **Measurement, Analysis and Knowledge Management Category** examines how your organization selects, gathers, analyses, manages, and improves its data, information, and knowledge assets. Also examined is how your organization reviews performance.

4.1a (1) Performance Measurement

(1) **How do you select, collect, align, and integrate data and information for tracking daily operations and for tracking overall organizational performance, including progress relative to strategic objectives and action plans? How do you use these data and information to support organizational decision making and innovation?**

RESPONSE FROM A SAMPLE LIBRARY APPLICATION

4.1a (1) DDL's focus is on developing and improving processes to support the core business of providing collections — i.e., library materials in all formats — to inform, educate and entertain. New technologies are being tested and adopted to enhance and to integrate the collection of information electronically. This step will enable the division to optimize its use of up-to-date information that supports operational and strategic decision-making and innovation. Figure 4.1–1 outlines some of the technologies that were/will be adopted for tracking daily operations and organizational performance.

Table 4.1a (1) Data and Information Collected to Track Daily Operations and Overall Performance and their impact on decision making

Technology	*Purpose*	*Impact on Decision Making*
Integrated Library Systems (ILS) [W]	• Combines library catalogs into a single-phase database — increase use of all resources (• Increase the breath and depth of collections through collaborative collection development policy • Real-time tracking of library resource (books, DVD, etc.) use. • Real-time tracking of customer requests unfilled (i.e., system did not find specific book title)	• See how collection use links with programming — receive additional ideas for programming that would be of interest to customers. • Compare with usage of other systems in other states Will be able to compare use of library materials by demographics, age, and education level — this will ensure that collections span all reading and education levels

Virtual Reference (24/7) [C]	24/7 — real time — customer to ask a reference question on the internet	Generates ideas for types of programming — by compiling the nature and subject of questions are about corporations in Delaware
Bibliostat Collect [C]	Collects statistical data on-line from public libraries, which are eventually imported into the FSCS national database. The federal database issues an annual report indicating the ranking of each state in key library operating functions.	The identification of Delaware's ranking as compared to other states on various data elements helps focus effort to improve on those rankings

CATEGORY 5—HUMAN RESOURCE FOCUS (90 POINTS)

The Human Resource Focus Category examines how your organization's work systems and employee learning and motivation enable employees to develop and utilize their full potential in alignment with your organization's overall objectives and action plans. Also examined are your organization's efforts to build and maintain a work environment and employee support climate conducive to performance excellence and to personal and organizational growth.

5.1a (1) How do you organize and manage work and jobs to promote cooperation, initiative, empowerment, innovation, and your organizational culture? How do you organize and manage work and jobs, including skills, to achieve the agility to keep current with business needs and to achieve your action plans?

RESPONSE FROM A SAMPLE LIBRARY APPLICATION

5.1a (1) Learning is the "business" of libraries, its fundamental mission and strategic imperative. As such, it is central to the discussion of 5.1a to acknowledge DDL as a learning organization. It is the core value of the agency and it permeates all levels of the organization. It is recognized that rewards and recognition lead to initiative, innovation and, ultimately, empowerment. Since 2000, DDL has actively practiced this value and pursued continuous quality improvement within the agency and the greater library community.

Senior leaders create an environment of empowerment and innovation by encouraging a learning organization and culture. In addition to workshops, an annual book is selected for the program, *If All The Delaware Library Community Read The Same Book ...* to encourage everyone to read a book that pertains to quality and innovation, and to set the stage so that individuals are more comfortable with change. Senior leaders share their learning and how they are applying it.

Quality principles and improvement tools have been applied to strategic planning, processes, customer focus, and human resource. Recommended workshops, to encourage a common learning experience, are listed in the DDL Professional Development chart, which documents participation by staff to date. Senior leaders also emphasize participation in interpersonal skills workshops to develop strong negotiating skills, to encourage good communication and teamwork, as well as to reinforce integrity and ethical behavior. Staff participates in training provided by the Office of State Personnel on Merit Rules and other ethical behavior for public servants.

Self-directed teams are formed to accomplish strategic goals and priorities, which create an environment conducive to organizational agility and innovation. For example, the DDL Quality Committee is a self-directed team, charged with the responsibility of bringing focus and direction to the quality project, completing an organizational self-assessment through submission of the Delaware Quality Award application, and monitoring and providing feedback in addressing opportunities for improvements. The senior leader has created a flat organization so employees can operate autonomously, defined boundaries and responsibilities, and shared authority and power. Communication lines are open in order to share information critical to good decision-making. Employees are provided with necessary resources, such as training and state-of-the art technology, to accomplish their collective goals. In essence, DDL's leadership and employees have created a vibrant performance management partnership.

CATEGORY 6—PROCESS MANAGEMENT (85 POINTS)

The **Process Management Category** examines the key aspects of your organization's process management, including key product, service, and business processes for creating customer and organizational value and key support processes. This Category encompasses all key processes and all work units.

6.1a (2) How do you determine key value creation process requirements, incorporating input from customers, suppliers, and partners, as appropriate? What are the key requirements for these processes?

RESPONSE FROM A SAMPLE LIBRARY APPLICATION

6.1a (2): Key Value Creation Process Requirements:
The consistent, disciplined processes, which the division employs in determining key value creation process requirements are the PDSA process (6.1–4), and the strategic planning process, which are aligned with the Balanced Scorecard objectives and goals.

Key Value Creation Process	*Key Performance Requirement*
Statewide Library Planning and Development	The improvement of libraries (national rankings by identifying and resolving problems with previous years' planning and library service processes. Meeting

(Key Value Creation Process)	*(Key Performance Requirement)*
	customer, supplier, staff and stakeholder needs.
State and Federal Funding	Accurate, timely, quality of annual budget and day-to-day financial transactions. Integrity of financial and reporting systems.
Collection Development	Ensuring collections meet customer demands.
Professional Development	Stakeholder, partner, and staff training to support quality and high-level library services.
DE Center for the Book	Providing targeted programming and lifelong learning opportunities to meet customer needs and wants.
Reference	Adequate and quality collection (books and other forms of information); up-to date technology; library staff training for providing reference services and quality customer service.

CATEGORY 7—BUSINESS RESULTS (450 POINTS)

The **Business Results Category** examines your organization's performance and improvement in key business areas-product and service outcomes, customer satisfaction, financial and marketplace performance, human resource results, operational performance, and leadership and social responsibility. Performance levels are relative to those of competitors.

7.1 Product and Service Results

7.1a What are your current levels and trends in key measures or indicators of product and service performance that are important to your customers? How do these results compare with your competitors' performance?

The figure on the left side of the page portrays the perceptions of patrons who used the services provided by the staff of the Library for the Blind and the Physically Handicapped (LBPH). Note that a clear majority of the respondents rated the services as either excellent or good (259 or 95%), compared with those who felt that they received services that were good or fair (15 or 5%). Not a single individual rated the services received as of "poor" quality. The figure on the right displays the assessment of patrons of libraries in the three counties of Delaware — Kent, Sussex and New Castle Counties appear to be rated highly by their customers, using eight factors to assess performance.

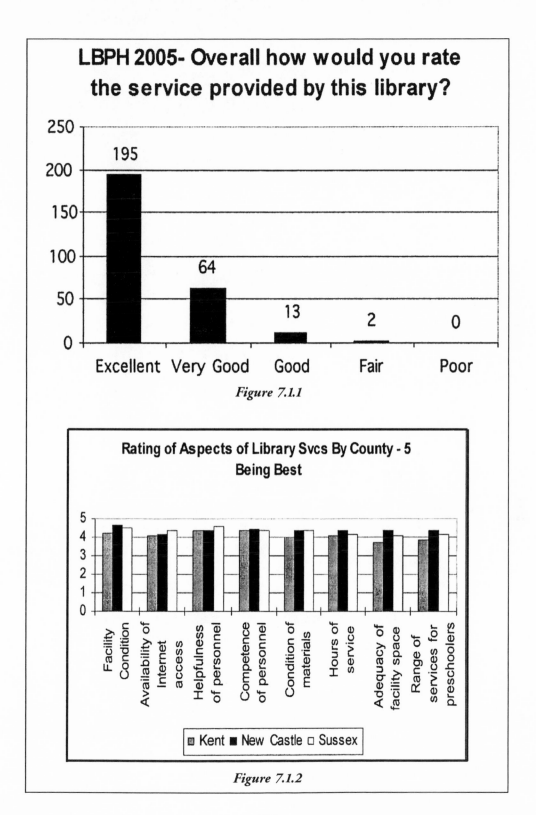

LBPH 2005- Overall how would you rate the service provided by this library?

Figure 7.1.1

Rating of Aspects of Library Svcs By County - 5 Being Best

Kent ■ New Castle □ Sussex

Figure 7.1.2

7.2 Customer-Focused Results

7.2a (1) What are your current levels and trends in key measures or indicators of customer satisfaction and dissatisfaction? How do these compare with competitors' level of customer satisfaction?

RESPONSE FROM A SAMPLE LIBRARY APPLICATION

7.2 Customer-Focused Results

The two figures displayed below show the level of customer satisfaction with the assistance provided by the staff of the Library for the Blind and the Physically Handicapped (LBPH). Ninety-four percent or 235 patrons indicated that they "almost always" or "always" received the assistance they requested (Figure 7.2.1) . In addition, 92% or 236 noted that staff members have been successful in finding solutions to their problems, as compared with less than 1% or two customers who claimed that the staff "never" found solutions to alleviate their problems (7.2.2).

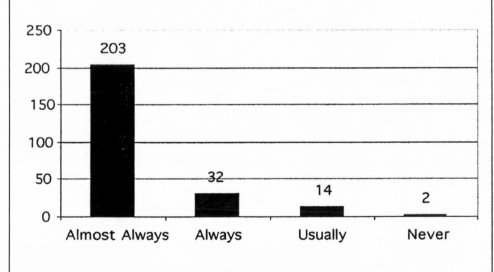

Figure 7.2.1

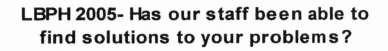

LBPH 2005- Has our staff been able to find solutions to your problems?

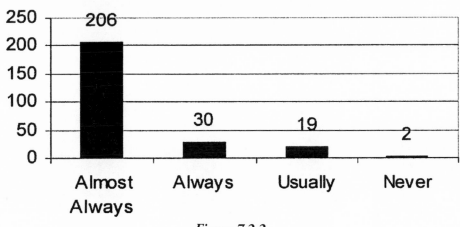

Figure 7.2.2

The charts below portray customers' opinions about the relative importance of libraries in improving the quality of their lives (Figure 7.2.3). A majority of the patrons (89%) expressed strong positive opinions on the importance of libraries, especially in Sussex County, the southern part of the state (Figure 7.2.4).

Customer's Opinion About Public Libraries

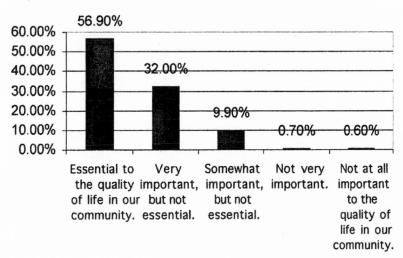

Figure 7.2.3

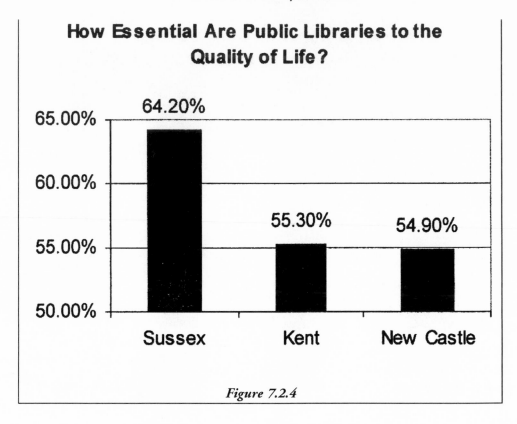

Figure 7.2.4

Part II

The Balanced Scorecard

9

Introduction to the Balanced Scorecard

"Even if you're on the right track, you'll get run over if you just sit there."
— Will Rogers

"What do I *do* with all of the numbers?! I'm an *English* major!" I whined.

Actually I'm also a Psychology major, so I can analyze why I'm so phobic about numbers. If I'd had forewarning that I'd lead an administration based on math, I would have run screaming in the opposite direction! But I have resigned myself to conquering numbers because it is essential to the success of libraries.

I've come to a somber realization that leaders in the library community must learn to use numbers for decision-making, in addition to using statistics to access funding dollars and to justify our existence. Intuitively, I believe that if we are managing our resources and services effectively we would be essential to the public and our value would be obvious. If we have to persuade people about our worth, then our worth is questionable.

The Balanced Scorecard

At long last, we discovered a tool for organizing all of the numbers! Basic spreadsheet and database tools weren't robust enough to capture and manipulate the amount of data that we were attempting to manage statewide. The Balanced Scorecard (BSC), our visual anchor, was developed by a Harvard professor and a business consultant to encourage organizations in expanding their focus beyond

This introduction was written by Anne E.C. Norman.

125

financial measures of success. They argued that performance measures of organizational effectiveness must also include metrics such as customer knowledge, internal processes, and learning and growth. The Balanced Scorecard is the tool used by the United Way, and has been adopted in part by the Institute of Museum and Library Services (IMLS) as Outcome Based Evaluation (OBE).

Our hope is that by using the entire Balanced Scorecard tool beginning with strategic objectives, lead and lag measures, strategic maps, and aligning all of our library processes, we will ultimately achieve stronger and more pervasive patron outcomes. We're developing our Balanced Scorecard as a visual tool for organizing and communicating strategic objectives and key measures so that everyone is clear on our strategic goals and can track improvements.

Statewide Master Plan for Library Services and Construction
Strategic Objectives

Expand and increase customers
Increase the capacity of buildings, hours of operation, and use of technologies
Develop staff competencies, leadership, and best practices
Greatest challenge — reduce the potpourri of governance

Delaware libraries have two million visits annually! Is that *good*? Two million sounds like a big number. Once I found out that less than half of Delawareans had a library card, I wondered if the number should be four million visits. But how many visits per cardholder indicate regular use? Maybe we should strive for eight million visits? Who knows? The following are some of the approaches we employed in answering the puzzling numbers and measurement questions that plagued us during the earlier stages of our performance improvement journey.

Frequency of Data

The Delaware Division of Libraries receives data once per year from the public libraries across the state through their annual reports. We then submit Delaware data for the National Center for Education statistics reports. But annually is not enough. Through our quality journey, we've learned that in order to affect change we need to examine the data frequently and consistently, at least on a quarterly basis.

In *The Agenda* by Michael Hammer, I discovered the importance of a single database. A single database is essential to foster collaboration among public libraries in collecting and using data to assess our collective performance. This approach assumes greater importance because public libraries in Delaware are governed and administered by different governmental entities. The following are a few concepts from Hammer's book:

- The (final) customer comes first
- The collaborative works together to serve the final customer
- The entire process should be designed as a unit
- All processes must be looked at in holistic terms
- No activity should be performed more than once
- Duplication of activities across all boundaries should be eliminated
- The entire collaborative should operate with one database
- Everyone shares the same version of all information

We established the Delaware Library Catalog, the core business tool for libraries, and invited all Delaware libraries to migrate into a single database. Phase I is completed when the existing database contains all of the public libraries in two out of three Delaware counties, all four libraries of the Delaware Technical and Community College campuses, Wesley College Library, and the Delaware Public Archives. Now that the Delaware Division of Libraries has access to the database, we can look under the hood to see how the collections are used across the entire library system. This approach will enable us to monitor our internal processes — to track collection usage, to support collaborative collection development, and to link collections with programming. When we all work together, including multitype libraries, we can support a deeper and broader collection that supports all educational levels. A single catalog also enables us to add innovative library technologies, which are too challenging to manage across various systems.

Six Sigma Lessons

One of the components of our quality-learning journey included training in Six Sigma. Two dozen librarians in Delaware are certified Six Sigma Green Belts. I recommend that Six Sigma training occur after a draft Balanced Scorecard is established. Six Sigma tools can be applied to analyzing the key measures that are captured in the Balanced Scorecard.

Understanding Variation by Donald Wheeler

Understanding Variation: The Key to Managing Chaos is a book by Donald Wheeler which explains that interpreting data is not about simply adding, subtracting, multiplying and dividing data, but about understanding how to digest the numbers to extract the knowledge that may be locked up inside the data. Information is random, but information is orderly.

An example of analysis that we've experimented with is applying variance analysis to circulation statistics. Now that we have live access to circulation data, we can examine emerging trends and test for improvements. We now understand that there is a threshold to variance; we understand when to ignore insignificant variation and at what point our efforts actually register improvement.

Customer Segmentation Study — Bundle and Target Services

The Institute for Learning Innovation is helping us to study the impact of libraries on lifelong learning, and conducted a pilot study on customer segmentation at the Dover Public Library. We are partnering with the Chief Officers of State Library Agencies (COSLINE) in the Northeast in this project, and we will use the results to bundle services for targeted customer groups to support them in achieving their goals.

State Aid Site Visits

How can the Delaware Division of Libraries help? How do we need to evolve state library services to support effective library development? As of June 2006, the Delaware Division of Libraries had obtained Balanced Scorecard software and populated it with data obtained through the Statewide Master Plan for Library Services & Construction. We are establishing the cause and effect linkages among the measures. Once we have a final draft, then we will use each library's BSC report to conduct site visits, to discuss what the library would like to focus on for improvements and how the Delaware Division of Libraries can help. I am expecting that we will learn from these visits how the Delaware Division of Libraries needs to evolve and improve services to truly support library development and excellence.

Synthesizing Collection and Programming Development

Currently, we are in the process of developing an integrated approach to collaborative collection development and programming development. Our premise is that the collections are our core business, and that library programming assists individuals with using the collections. Our collections and programming need to reflect the learning paths of Delawareans. We intend to conduct a needs assessment to determine the outcomes that we are striving for, and then develop a rubric for self-directed learning to capture the outcomes that are achieved. Outcome Based Evaluation, as required by IMLS, will be an important addition to our Balanced Scorecard once we develop our approach.

The succeeding section of the book on the Balanced Scorecard was written by Despina Dapias Wilson, our management analyst at the Delaware Division of Libraries. Despina shares my passion for learning about business best practices and in recent years she completed dual Master's degrees in Business Administration and Public Administration. As librarians, we need to learn to allow other types of professionals to help us. Libraries in Delaware are benefiting tremendously from Despina's knowledge and experience as she applies her professional best practices to them. She compiled and wrote our second application for the Delaware Quality Award assessment process, articulating our improvements to date and for which the Delaware Division of Libraries received the Delaware Quality Award of Merit.

Recommended Readings

The Balanced Scorecard: Translating Strategy into Action by Robert S. Kaplan and David P. Norton (1996)

The Strategy Focused Organization, by Robert S. Kaplan and David P. Norton (2001)

Strategy Maps, by Robert S. Kaplan and David P. Norton (2004)

Insights to Performance Excellence 2005: An Inside Look at the 2005 Baldrige Award Criteria, Mark Blazey (2005).

10

The History, Purpose, and Definitions of the Balanced Scorecard

"Change is the law of life. And those who look only to the past and the present are certain to miss the future."
— President John F. Kennedy

So far, what has been unveiled — through the step-by-step explanation of the Baldrige Criteria in Part I — is the framework of a quality organization. The purpose of going through this assessment process is to give a holistic view of where your organization stands as far as its strengths, weaknesses, opportunities and threats (SWOT). Metaphorically, it is like opening a toy chest and laying out all the Lego pieces on the floor (SWOT results). Now that all the separate pieces are visible on the floor, it becomes easier to start organizing them by color, design, and size. If our goal is to build a fort within 10 minutes (objective), we would first need to have a vision of what this fort would look like (vision), then determine the strategy we will have to use to build it in the most efficient and effective way (strategy and measures, i.e., which pieces we need to use, how many pieces, how they must be combined to construct a strong and well-designed fort).

This example, although over simplified, is analogous to building a Balanced Scorecard. The BSC is an integrated framework that organizes information into stratospheres called Perspectives, which forces the alignment of objectives, measures, targets, initiatives, and results with the organization's strategic plan, mission and vision. Think of the Baldrige Criteria as a map and the Balanced Scorecard as a compass.

Chapter 10 through 14 were written by Despina Dapias Wilson.

Background and History of Measurement

Measurement or fact-based management is not a new approach to assessing performance. During and after World War II, management started using company data to drive performance improvement — one company that did this was the Ford Motor Company. However, the systems used were reflective of an industrial age which is now largely obsolete and irrelevant to the information society.

Dr. W. E. Deming (1950s)

In the 1950s, a new form of management started to emerge with the work of W. Edwards Deming. He was the statistician who had first introduced quality management to the United States, although it was not well received at that time. It can be hypothesized that the reason for its poor reception was that industrial age strategies were so well ingrained in the American way of doing business so that any new style was seen as unconventional and unproductive. Deming took his theory to Japan where it was adopted immediately. Deming's work introduced the concepts of quality, innovation, and employee empowerment. He also highlighted the importance of customer feedback and measurement-based management.

The approach used during the industrial age was based on the idea that in order to guarantee quality products to the customer, the products should be inspected and tested when produced, and again before they went out for consumption. Deming believed that this process was flawed, that the true causes of product defects could not be detected at the end of production. At that point it may be too late to fix the product, causing much waste of time, dollars and resources. Instead, if the production process were monitored every step of the way, any variations possibly causing defects could be identified and addressed immediately. This would allow for better management and distribution of people, money, equipment and other resources. He called this a feedback loop and named the process Plan-Do-Study-Act (PDSA).

Others who followed Deming developed modified theories, but Deming was the only one who believed that the foundation and most integral part of innovation and quality improvement are the employees.

TQM (1987)

After seeing, reading about and experiencing the successes that Japanese companies were having by implementing the Deming theory, organizations in the United States decided to follow suit. In 1987, the Deming philosophy was applied to two initiatives, one in the military arena and one in the civilian. The military initiative was launched by the Department of Defense, which brought about significant changes to policies, the introduction of Management by Objectives, and the simplification of their acquisition process. The civilian initiative came to be known as the Baldrige Award.

Malcolm Baldrige, who was the first secretary of commerce under Ronald Reagan, was struck by the significant success that Japanese companies were enjoying. Baldrige saw Deming's theory as the answer to revitalizing America's competitiveness. A carefully-designed questionnaire was developed; it queried on vital and multiple aspects of a well-run, quality organization, and gained prominence as the Baldrige Criteria. Instead of monetary incentives, a prestigious award would be presented annually to winning organizations at a high profile ceremony in Washington, D.C. The winning organizations benefited from the publicity and were required to talk about their success stories as a best practice case to help other organizations, nationally and internationally.

Winning the Baldrige Award has been a good predictor of and has benefited the stock performance of winning companies. The trend shows that the overall growth of winners is greater the common market indices, including the S&P 500 (see Figure 1).

However, what had plagued managers in all industries were the confusion and the lack of knowledge of what kind of measurement system to use. By posing questions in seven key areas, the Baldrige self assessment provides answers that help organizations to better understand how well they are performing but it does not recommend what kind of measurement system should be used. This is why the early winners and the majority of the winners of the Baldrige Award were mainly private sector companies. The private sector has traditionally had some form of systematic performance measurement method in place to track sales quotas and bottom line financial results. Eventually, the government and not-for-profit organizations were mandated by the Government Performance and Results Act of 1993 (GPRA) to modify the way they do business, to be more accountable, and to design a performance management system. This was the watershed year when government agencies had to get serious about justifying their existence to maintain funding levels.

Balanced Scorecard (BSC) (1990s)

The Balanced Scorecard was originally developed in the early 1990s by Harvard professor Robert S. Kaplan and management consultant David P. Norton. They started studying a dozen companies to determine what would constitute a new and credible method of measuring organizational performance. What they discovered was that companies — despite the emphasis on quality — still relied heavily on financial measures to determine the success of their organizations. However, financial measures represented just a fraction of the whole picture. To be able to determine the success of an organization, Kaplan and Norton concluded that additional critical components were necessary to be able to create value for the organization. These components were: focus on the customer, the efficiency and effectiveness of internal processes, and most of all, the well-being and empowerment of its employees — all key to the success of the organization's mission, vision, and strategy.

Since the methodology has gained the attention of the business community, over half of the *Fortune* 1000 organizations have adopted it. The Balanced Scorecard approach can be easily adopted by the public sector. The reason is that it does not rely so heavily on financial performance; rather it aligns mission and strategy with action plans. This is why so many government agencies have started implementing the BSC as a good way of meeting the requirements of the Government Performance Results Act (GPRA). The Institute of Museum and Library Services (IMLS), as a federal agency, must abide by GPRA, and the way state and local governments must report to IMLS is affected as well.

Why Should Libraries Use the Balanced Scorecard?

There are three important reasons that support libraries' use of the Balanced Scorecard

Demonstrate Accountability

There is no doubt that there is a value proposition associated with libraries. According to the statewide master plan, 92 to 98 percent of Delaware users and non-users of libraries reported that libraries are essential to enhancing the quality of life.

Until recently, it seemed that libraries never needed to justify their existence. However, times and economies are changing and funding bodies, as well as tax-payers, are demanding to see greater returns on investment.

In government, however, funding is generally made available based upon the mission of an agency or the reason it was created in the first place, irrespective of its performance. For example, funding for a fire department is likely to be increased for training and hiring despite the fact that this need could be attributed to poor performance. This is totally the opposite of what would occur in the private sector. So what is all this business about accountability and the GPRA? The answer is that governments must be accountable as stewards of taxpayer money. To be more accountable, agencies must create a more mission-effective and mission-efficient government. Delaware, for example, is enjoying a AAA+ bond rating because of its prudent financial accountability. This means that savings are passed on to taxpayers who pay less interest on state issued bonds. But back to libraries ...

Library professionals are supposed to be experts when it comes to organizing information; yet, while they have always collected data, it hasn't been expressly for decision-making or performance improvement.

Library schools have not prepared their graduates to do strategic planning, data-based decision making, and evaluation of organizational performance because management and business courses are not requirements. Without being too critical one way or the other, we can undoubtedly say that this may be one of many reasons why libraries are experiencing a lag in the information industry today.

Most graduates of reputable library schools typically move up to managerial and leadership positions, without formal training in the business field, and are asked to perform tasks that school did not prepare them for. For example, state librarians, by virtue of their leadership roles, have to possess the skills of politicians, the competencies of budget experts, and the vision of strategic planners. They have to set measurable objectives, identify tasks, and strategic goals. They are asked to supervise and lead people, and to track their employees' performance as well as their organizational performance. These are complex and multiple competencies that are often difficult to find in a single executive.

Librarians today are asked to provide quality services and products by applying quality principles, such as visionary and transformational leadership, a strong customer focus, well-trained and highly motivated employees, a systematic knowledge management system, and effective and efficient processes. Most of all, they are expected to produce quality results and outcomes.

We are now, more than ever, living in a rapidly changing and growing information society. This development puts libraries in the middle of the storm because libraries are in the business of providing information. Lately, this information has to be in an electronic and virtual format. Today's information-savvy consumers need information now, where it's easily accessible, accurate, up to date, and in their preferred format. Details, customization and differentiation play a big role. How can libraries differentiate themselves? Private industries have thrived on this and have literally created huge virtual cafés, and have become information powerhouses. According to Dr. Mark L. Blazey, president of the Quantum Performance Group, the average shelf life of new knowledge today is about five years, whereas in the year 2020 it will be 38 days.

It seems that libraries have almost missed the boat on the information wave.

They thought they were prepared, but in reality they are having a very challenging time catching up with the Googles and the Amazon.coms. Granted, one of the problems that libraries face is the protection of patron privacy. In order to preserve individual privacy, libraries have to purge huge amounts of operational data on a regular basis. For example, libraries have to purge information on the books a patron checks out, which identifies that person's interests — both are critical details for libraries to have when deciding which books to buy. At the same time, funding agencies expect libraries to justify their existence with more data and outcome-based results. The ability to collect data to support decision-making and to be accountable must be balanced with the right to privacy of citizens.

We are happy to say that more and more libraries are moving toward obtaining data warehouses like the Normative Data Project (NDP database) to help with "patron use data" attached to demographics instead of individuals. Libraries must move fast, be smart, and act, right now.

To illustrate the speed at which we have to move and the consequences of not doing so, let us take the example of another industry that found itself in a similar situation — and ironically is in the private sector: the automotive industry in the early 1970s. The automotive industry was resting on its laurels until the gasoline crisis ended its complacency. Japanese car manufacturers were producing smaller, more gas efficient cars and literally steamrolled the American industry. Consumer Reports noted that a three-year-old American-made vehicle typically has as may problems as an eight-year-old Asian model. This translates into a five-year lag in quality. And this is private industry! Imagine how this compares to the pace of public libraries or government in general.

Accountability is no longer a choice but a requirement. The Balanced Scorecard *is* a better way of evaluating and monitoring organizational performance because it provides focus and accountability. It's an effective tool in linking objectives with strategy implementation. Intuition and anecdotal data need to be supported with strategic measures and results to enhance credibility and effectiveness. In the majority of cases, the hard-core library metrics that are currently collected nationwide cannot be characterized as strategic, because every library agency is a unique entity with different sets of customer requirements, key processes, human resource and technology needs, and varying priorities.

Function as a Business

Government agencies can benefit immensely by trying to operate like a business and by following common business practices. Although government agencies deal with "softer" issues, which involve people, instead of "harder" issues like manufacturing cars, there are many similarities. Both have the responsibility of being accountable to their customers.

Table 10.1 translates the differences and similarities between the private and public sectors as illustrated by Paul Arveson from the Balanced Scorecard Institute.

Table 10.1 Comparing Strategic Features: Private and Public Sector Organizations		
Strategic Feature	*Private Sector*	*Public Sector*
General Strategic Goal	Competitiveness	Mission effectiveness
	Innovaation; creativity; good	Accountability to public;
General financial goals	Profit growth; market share	Cost reduction; efficiency
Values	will; recognition	Integrity; fairness
Desired Outcome	Customer satisfaction	Customer satisfaction
Stakeholders	Stockholders; owners; market	Taxpayers; inspectors; legislators
Budget Priorities	Customer demand	Leadership; legislators; planners
Defined by: Justification for secrey	Protection of intellectual capital; proprietary knowledge	National security
Key Success Factors	Growth rate; earnings; market share	Best management practices
	Uniqueness	Sameness; economies of scale
	Advanced technology	Standardized technology

Despite their perceived differences, both sectors consider customer satisfaction as a worthy outcome and a strategic imperative. This translation is a necessary step when trying to determine what constitutes success in the private and public sectors and what the unifying focus should be when developing a measurement system.

Open the Door to a New Way of Doing Strategic Planning

Kaplan and Norton have devoted much of their writing to strategy maps to illustrate the cause and effect relationship of the performance goals and objectives and how the overall infrastructure of a strategic plan greatly affects the mission of the organization. For libraries, as is the case for businesses and most public agencies, the ultimate goal is customer loyalty, retention, and satisfaction. This approach emphasizes the importance of aligning what we say with what we actually do.

In the side-by-side comparison below (Table 10.2), we can see how developing and applying a strategic plan (i.e., the BSC approach) evolves from a five-year process to a fully integrated plan that is embedded into in the everyday operation of an organization.

Table 10.2 Old vs. New Ways of Strategic Planning. Adapted from Paul Arveson, "The Revolution in Strategic Planning" (Balanced Scorecard Institute, 2004.)

How Strategic Planning Was or Still Is	How BSC Can Evolve Strategic Planning
Typical strategic planning cycle is five years. Evaluation takes place every four years.	By monitoring, mapping, and reviewing the strategy on a real-time basis, strategy can be revised as necessary at any point in time, and is evaluated "just in time" to make sure managers are not just doing it right but doing the right things.
Planning is done by one or two senior leaders with minimal interaction and feedback from staff. Planning is done without analyzing the internal and external organizational environment, and with no outside help. No structure to the plan.	All staff is involved in the strategic planning process. Analysis of strengths, weaknesses, threats and opportunities are sought from outside professionals. Best practices are incorporated. The BSC framework is used for consistency, alignment, and prioritization.
Learning and growth are minimally incorporated and do not stimulate innovation. Major changes do not occur and plans tend to be repetitive with little or no benchmarking.	Employees at all levels are empowered (i.e., equipped with the right tools and knowledge to do their jobs). They are assigned targeted measures, form cross-functional teams and know precisely what to do to get to the next level of performance in the strategic plan.
"If it ain't broke, don't fix it."	Innovation and creative strategic thinking are encouraged at all levels.
The goal is to meet mandated reporting standards.	The goal is to exceed reporting standards and to exceed customer expectations.

How Strategic Planning Was or Still Is	How BSC Can Evolve Strategic Planning
The five-year plan is just a flat, mandated and sometimes complicated document, with a "cookie-cutter" structure.	The strategic plan takes the form of colorful strategy maps, with cause and effect arrows, interconnecting goals and objectives, showing at a glance the infrastructure that will make success possible. The strategy map focuses on four or five themes and is comprehensive.
The strategic plan sits on a shelf.	The strategic plan is a living document and an everyday map, which guides the day's direction. It is an interactive and dynamic tool. It is tied into the staff performance plans and promotes manager accountability.
In the majority of the cases, no alignment between mission, vision, strategy, objectives and measures. Performance measures tend to be ad-hoc.	BSC strategic performance measures force the alignment with the mission and vision.
Managers tend to focus on short-term financial goals. Customer goals are not targeted to market needs.	The BSC balances and aligns performance measures and expectations between and among major perspectives (Customer, Internal Processes, Knowledge and Growth, and Financial).
Data Rich, Information Poor (D.R.I.P.). Analysis paralysis.	The BSC forces organizations to determine and focus on what really matters to achieve success. Decision-making is directly linked to pertinent data and measures. Data dashboards provide real-time performance. Analysis, not paralysis.
Planning is project-oriented: not necessarily having targeted outcomes in mind.	Planning is results-oriented: keeps the outcome in mind throughout the planning process. Strategic measures help monitor progress of outcomes.
Doing things right.	Doing the right things.
Performance reporting not systematic and non-existent in many cases. Performance reports not visible to all levels of an organization.	Performance reporting is systematic, just in time for decision-making and is visible to all levels of an organization as a communication tool.

How Strategic Planning Was or Still Is	How BSC Can Evolve Strategic Planning
The execution of the budget is not aligned with performance measures (if any), and in most cases not aligned with strategic plans.	Budgets are directly linked to the outcome of each perspective and are guided by performance measures.
Reactive collection of performance measures. Some measures not needed, but collected just in case. Simply collect data.	Proactive collection of performance measures. All measures have a purpose and are collected systematically and continuously throughout the organization just in time. Analyze data.
Employee performance reviews disconnected from strategic plan. Provides unclear or no plan of what to change/adjust if targets are not met.	Employee performance plans are directly linked to performance measures. Provides a clear plan of what to change/adjust if targets are not met.

Why Is It Called "Balanced"?

- It weighs and balances other non-financial operational components, referred to as Perspectives. All are essential to the success of the organization's ultimate objective, whether it is to make more money, or to create greater value for its customers.
- It balances and aligns short- and long-term goals. Measures can be set to monitor progress by time intervals.
- It balances outputs and outcomes or lag and lead measures. A lag measure reflects an outcome or bottom-line results. A lead measure is a predictor of future behavior or performance, and is considered a performance driver. A typical lag measure is customer satisfaction. It is a measure of all the things the organization has done at the end of a time period and reflects a focus on hard-core results. A typical lead measure may be the number of outreach activities. The logic behind this is that the more people are informed about what libraries do and offer, the greater the chances of increasing customer satisfaction because you are increasing the library's visibility and accessibility to patrons. This makes the number of outreach events a lead measure that drives customer satisfaction, the lag measure.

For years libraries have been collecting mostly output measures because they are easier to collect, and, in most cases, are readily available. The Institute of Museum and Library Services (IMLS) has been pushing for outcomes via the Outcomes Based Evaluation (OBE) model because there has been an increasing demand for accountability from public agencies to justify their LSTA appropriation. OBE can be a great resource for lag measures.

- It achieves balance between the external and internal operating components of the organization: Financial and Customer perspectives representing the external components (shareholders/stakeholders and customers), and Processes and Learning and Growth representing the internal components (staff and internal processes).

- It balances and aligns all the measures of the organization with its mission, vision, values, and strategies.

- It balances strategy development with strategy deployment; in other words, actions and results. Libraries are experts at telling a good story. Many have inspiring visions and compelling strategies, but are often unaligned with employee actions. The BSC not only helps in developing a focused strategy but links employee ownership of measures every step of the way. This way, employees know at any point in time what to do to get to the next level.

What Is a Balanced Scorecard?

The BSC is a comprehensive management system that clarifies, balances and aligns an organization's vision and strategy, and translates them into actions through the use of linked performance measures in four perspectives. It is more than a simple measurement tool. Most important, it provides senior executives with the ability to periodically monitor progress in achieving the organization's strategic goals.

In the classic BSC, there are four Perspectives and their typical order is Customer, Financial, Internal Processes, and Learning and Growth. The strategic plan is stratified among the four perspectives, with strategic objectives and with related measures and their targets. Key initiatives are then associated with each strategic objectives and are assigned their respective budgets.

Kaplan and Norton describe why the Balanced Scorecard is an innovation worthy of the information age:

> The balanced scorecard retains traditional financial measures. But financial measures tell the story of past events, an adequate story for industrial age companies for which investments in long-term capabilities and customer relationships were not critical for success. These financial measures are inadequate, however, for guiding and evaluating the journey

that information age companies must make to create future value through investment in customers, suppliers, employees, processes, technology, and innovation [http://www.balancedscorecard.org/basics/bsc1.html].

Table 10.3
Illustrates the Linear Format
of a Balanced Scorecard

		STRATEGY MAP	BALANCED SCORECARD				ACTION PLAN			
Vision and Mission	Strategic Themes	Strategy: Improve Stakeholder Value	<u>Financial</u> "To succeed financially, how should we appear to our stakeholders?"	Objectives	Measures	Targets	Initiatives	Owner(s) & Monitors	Budget	OUTPUTS OUTCOMES → RESULTS
		Strategy: Create Value for Our Customers (Retain & Acquire)	<u>Customers</u> "To achieve our vision, how should we appear to our customers?"	Objectives	Measures	Targets	Initiatives	Owner(s) & Monitors	Budget	
		Strategy: Innovation, Customer Management, Operational Excellence	<u>Internal Process</u> "To satisfy our stakeholders and customers, what business processes must we excel at?"	Objectives	Measures	Targets	Initiatives	Owner(s) & Monitors	Budget	
		Strategy: Develop Culture for Lifelong Learning & Coaching	<u>Learning and Growth</u> "To achieve our vision, how will we sustain our ability to improve and grow?"	Objectives	Measures	Targets	Initiatives	Owner(s) & Monitors	Budget	

Table 10.3 Framework of the Balanced Scorecard Management System.

The selection and prioritization of the four perspectives depends on the organization's mission and strategy. The four perspectives are linked by cause and effect relationships and are interdependent. They are the guideposts by which metrics are developed and data are collected and analyzed. The Division of Libraries opted to prioritize the perspectives in this order: Customer, Internal Processes, Knowledge and Growth, and Financial. Before we delve into each perspective, we should clarify some of the Balanced Scorecard key concepts and terminology.

Understanding Balanced Scorecard Terminology

Cascading

One of the findings of the Himmel, Wilson, & Providence report was that a multitude of factors were responsible for Delaware's low national rankings. It appears that the problem stemmed from a lack of alignment of strategic objectives and measures between DDL and the public libraries. As a way to ensure that DDL and public libraries all have the same unifying vision, mission, and strategy, they recommended various, interdependent levels of balanced scorecards that would start at the top (state) level, and cascade down into interlinking "sub" scorecards supporting the top (Figure 10.1). As you can deduce from the DDL experience, cascading is the process of developing aligned scorecards at every level of the organization. Think of the overall scorecard as the destination and all the cascaded scorecards as the little side roads that lead to that destination. As an example, when we visit Mapquest online, we know the destination, but do not know how to get there. The map and the step-by-step driving directions provide us with the direc-

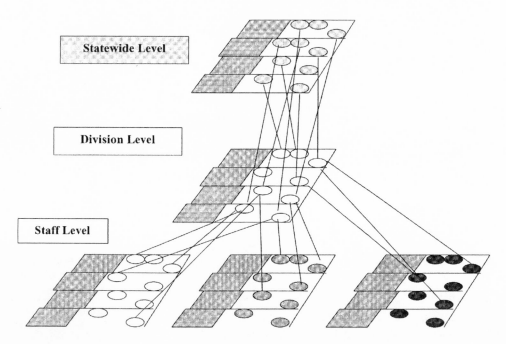

Table 10.1 *Cascading Effects of Strategy Maps. Source: Adapted from Bill Barberg, Insight-formation.*

tions that will help us get to our destination. This is exactly the relationship between the overall scorecard and those that cascade down from it.

Cascaded scorecards often differ with and within each level of the organization (Figure 10.1). What is measured at the state level may not necessarily be measured at the division or staff levels. The same thinking applies when developing cascaded scorecards for the strategy map (i.e., when creating the cause and effect relationships, where the objectives from the lower levels link to the higher levels). For example, if we take the subject of training, the planning team may measure the number of training sessions planned for the public libraries, while the IT staff's objectives and measures may relate to ensuring the availability of appropriate computer and video equipment and the infrastructure set-up needed to carry out the training. These objectives and measures collectively provide professional development opportunities to the customers (i.e., the public libraries) and therefore contribute to the overall statewide strategic objectives of recruiting and retaining qualified staff, and developing required competencies within the Learning and Growth perspective.

Key Performance Indicators (KPI)

These refer to the vital few measures that are key to the overall success of the organization in achieving its mission and strategic priorities.

Knowledge Management

This represents the collective knowledge and cumulative experiences of an organization and the communication infrastructure in place to share organizational knowledge. It includes not only the knowledge obtained via training and professional development, but also how knowledge and information is disseminated across all levels of the organization. It also includes the creative and effective ways that knowledge is applied by the employees who completed the training.

Measures

Every strategic objective should have a measure associated with it that will reveal if we are making progress toward achieving that objective. The term "measures" is sometimes substituted for "performance indicator." A measure for "expand customer base" could be "number of unique library card holders," and a measure for "retain existing customers" could be "number of customers who have previously attended programs." While developing measures we must always keep in mind to "balance" lead and lag measures.

Non-value–added Work

Non-value–added work refers to activities that do not add any value to the process and ultimately do little or nothing to satisfy customers. Such activities are often not necessary, and could be eliminated. Multiple levels of approvals before an invoice can be processed and paid is a good example of a non-value-added step.

Objectives

The scorecard terminology for objectives is "strategic objectives." They are also referred to as "strategic goals" or "performance objectives." These objectives describe how the strategies will be achieved, and as Paul R. Niven points out, "are more precise and specific than strategies, but less granular than measures." They are typically expressed in a verb-adjective-noun phrase. Examples of strategic or performance objectives are: "expand customer base" or "strengthen customer trust, loyalty, and confidence." When developing these objectives, it is important to keep in mind that they should be linked in cause and effect relationships that cross through the multiple scorecard perspectives — visually illustrated in what is known as a strategy map.

Performance-based Budgeting

In performance-based budgeting, funds are directly aligned with and distributed to specific initiatives and are adjusted based on the performance rate. A poor performance can mean a proportionate reduction in funds for that initiative.

Performance Indicators

A performance indicator is a particular value or characteristic used to measure output or outcome.

Perspectives

The traditional Perspectives are Financial, Customer, Internal Processes, and Knowledge and Growth. In the private sector, the highest Perspective is Financial. For the government and the non-profit sector, the Customer Perspective is elevated to the top and is focused on the mission-driven nature of public agencies. The objectives within each perspective are interdependent and are linked together in a chain of cause and effect relationships. Sometimes, libraries or government entities have a tendency to limit focus to the customer and ignore the other perspectives, such as Financial and Knowledge and Growth. Libraries also need to consider the three other Perspectives to achieve performance excellence and exceed their patrons' expectations for public library services and products.

The four Perspectives are framed based on the responses to the following specific questions:

- The Financial Perspective asks: "To succeed financially, how should we appear to our stakeholders?"
- The Customer Perspective asks: "To achieve our vision, how should we appear to our customers?"
- The Internal Processes Perspective asks: "To satisfy our stakeholders and customers, what processes must we excel at?"
- Learning and Growth Perspective, which focuses on human capital, technology and organizational culture — the intangible assets that create value — asks: "To achieve our vision, how will we sustain our ability to change and improve?"

Return on Investment (ROI)

In the public sector, return on investment represents the difference between the cost benefit or savings received after an improved service and the actual cost of the service. Let's consider this hypothetical example: In a public library in rural Delaware, for every dollar spent in libraries, the community receives six dollars back in services. This indicates a return equivalent to six times the initial investment; the higher the ROI, the more valuable the services.

Stakeholders

These are individuals or groups that support, influence, and have a stake in the organization's success. They may be legislators, representatives, other state agencies that have oversight duties, and members of the community that represent the interests of the public (i.e., friends of libraries).

Strategic Initiatives

These are basically initiatives that the libraries often contract with outside organizations to achieve and are designed to specifically accomplish part of the strategy or help reach a certain target. For example, in Delaware, the Division of Libraries contracted the help of library consultants Himmel & Wilson, Providence Associates to implement a year-long study — the Statewide Master Plan Study — to help determine the current status of the state's public library infrastructure for construction, services and library standards. Initiatives almost always have start dates and end dates. Strategic initiatives must be focused and purposeful, meaning that they must be integrally related and aligned to a particular objective. If too many operational tasks are identified as strategic initiatives, it becomes challenging to set priorities and stay focused on the critical targets.

Strategy Map

This is a multidimensional illustration showing an organization's strategy through a series of objectives that are interdependent and have a cause and effect relationship. Figure 10.2 illustrates a strategy map.

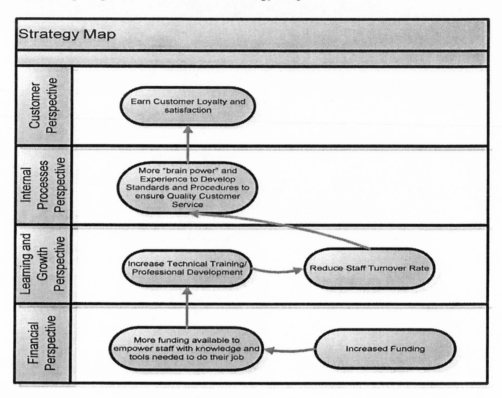

Figure 10.2 *Example of Strategy Map.*

Strategic Themes

These are also called Key Success Factors (KSF). They usually are four to five overarching priority areas that the organization focuses its resources on in order to achieve its vision. For the Delaware Division of Libraries the strategic objectives are: library development, collaboration, sustainability, resource management, life-long learning.

SWOT Analysis

This can be synonymous to an environmental scan. The acronym stands for Strengths, Weaknesses (internal), Opportunities and Threats (external). The SWOT analysis is a planning exercise in which senior leaders identify organizational strengths and weaknesses, and environmental opportunities and threats. Based on this analysis, leaders select the best strategic priorities (themes or goals) to achieve the mission and vision.

Targets

Targets are the levels of performance we intend to accomplish based on benchmarking or other analysis. We can have *short-term* targets, which are usually the ones to be achieved within the first fiscal year, *interim* targets that are to be achieved in the second and third years, and *long-term* targets that are to be achieved in the fourth and fifth years. All these can be reflected accordingly, by priority order, in the Balanced Scorecard. A stretch target is one that is set at a value higher than what is expected. This is done to mainly test the system and to force innovation and breakthrough performance.

In an automated BSC, target results can be color-coded for ease of interpretation in a quick and accurate manner. Traditionally, red identifies all the missed targets, yellow means that we are progressing or getting closer to the target, and green identifies all the targets that have been met or exceeded.

Value

Value refers to benefit per unit cost or what is known as "per capita" calculation.

Value-added-work

Value-added-work refers to activities that add value to a process or service. Value-added activities are efficient at getting to the desired result (as opposed to non-value-added work and repetition). They are perceived by the customers as valuable because they help control costs, thus increasing customer satisfaction.

11

Components of a
Balanced Scorecard

"All men by nature desire knowledge."
— Aristotle (384 B.C.-
322 B.C.)

What Does a Balanced
Scorecard Look Like?

Now that we have completed an overview of what the BSC is and clarified some of its terminology, we will break down each section and briefly describe what it is and what it looks like.

Strategy Map

This is an "at-a-glance" management tool that can be used by all levels of an organization. As defined earlier, this is an actual illustration of the mapped, interdependent objectives, stratified by perspective, and interlinked by their cause and effect relationship. This is like "flowcharting" the organization's strategy from the bottom up. An example of what a sample strategy map looks like is given below (Fig. 11.1). (See Figure 13.2 for the DDL strategy map).

Perspectives

The first column represents the four perspectives in the order of their relationship to the organizational strategy map. DDL's order is Customer, Internal Processes, Knowledge and Innovation, and Financial.

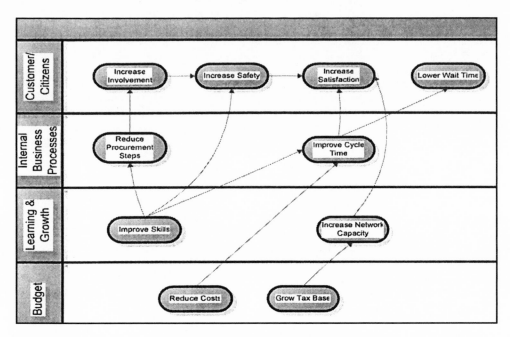

Figure 11.1 *Example of a Public Sector Strategy Map. Source: Adapted from Howard Rohm, "Improve Public Sector Results with a Balanced Scorecard," http://www.balancescorecard.org.*

Strategic Objectives

The second column identifies the strategic objectives of the organization. These objectives can be taken directly from the strategy map. This is why we need to

Perspective	Strategic Objectives
Customer	Expand customer base
	Retain existing customers
	Create value for customers
Internal Processes	Optimize facilities
	Improve resources
	Enhance access
Knowledge and Innovation	Recruit and retain qualified staff
	Develop required competencies
	Develop leadership
	Foster innovation
Financial	Encourage local investment
	Streamline governance
	Create developmental policies

develop the strategy map first, where all the cause and effect linkages and objectives are identified and consensus is achieved. DDL's objectives are:

Strategic Measures

The third and fourth columns list specific measures for each objective and identifies it as a lead or lag measure. It is important to keep in mind that you need a balance between the lead and lag measures. DDL's measures look like this:

Perspective	Strategic Objectives	Measures	Type
Customer	Expand customer base	Registered borrowers as a percent of the service population	Lag
	Retain existing customers	Repeat program registrants	Lag
	Create value for customers	Number of promotional events Customer satisfaction rate	Lead Lag
Internal Processes	Optimize facilities	Facilities use rate	Lead
	Improve resources Enhance access	Total collections per capita Average age of collection Number of training facilities Number of assistive technologies implemented Number of computer workstations /100 people	Lag Lead Lead Lag Lag
Knowledge and Innovation	Recruit and retain qualified staff	Staff retention rate Number and percent of staff attending training	Lag Lead
	Develop required competencies	Number of staff using scholarship program to Obtain MLS	Lead
	Develop leadership & foster innovation	Number of programming best practice kits adopted	Lead
Financial	Encourage local investment	Total local operating income capita	Lag
	Streamline governance	Number of libraries in county system	Lag

(Perspective)	(Strategic Objectives)	(Measures)	(Type)
	Create developmental policies	Percent of libraries with collection development policy	Lead
		Percent of libraries w/internet use policy	Lead

Although rare, there may be instances where some objectives do not appear to have appropriate measures. If this is the situation, it is sometimes beneficial to keep such objectives on the scorecard as a placeholder and discussion point. After further analysis, you and your team might decide to either keep or discard those tentative measures. Also, it is not true that each measure should have lead and lag measures. Furthermore, the balance of lead and lag measures should be counted as an overall total on the scorecard and not separately per Perspective.

Sometimes, especially during the early phases of development of a scorecard, the lag measures tend to be greater in number than the lead measures. This is acceptable as long as the total number balances out at the end. As the BSC becomes refined, the lead and lag measures tend to naturally balance out more.

Performance Data

The fifth column is for performance data, which can reflect results from various time periods (daily, monthly, or quarterly).

Perspective	Strategic Objectives	Measures	Type	Actual
Customer	Expand customer base	Registered borrowers as a percent of the service population	Lag	62%
	Retain existing customers	Percent repeat program registrants	Lag	25%
	Create value for customers	Number of promotional events	Lead	5
		Customer satisfaction rate	Lag	89%
Internal Processes	Optimize facilities	Facilities use rate	Lead	33%
	Improve resources	Total collections per capita	Lag	2.5
		Average age of collection	Lead	6.25 years
	Enhance access	Number of training facilities	Lead	1

(Perspective)	(Strategic Objectives)	(Measures)	(Type)	(Actual)
		Number of assistive technologies implemented	Lag	4
		Number of computer workstations/100 pop.	Lead	.25
Knowledge and Innovation	Recruit and retain qualified staff	Staff retention rate	Lag	98%
		Percent of staff attending training	Lead	62%
	Develop required competencies	Number of staff using scholarship program to obtain MLS	Lead	2
	Develop leadership	Number of programming best practice kits adopted	Lead	28
Financial	Encourage local investment	Total local operating income per capita	Lag	$20.28
		Total local capital expenditures per capita	Lag	$.52
	Streamline governance	Number of libraries in county systems	Lag	13
	Create developmental policy	Percent of libraries with collection development policy	Lead	87%
		Percent of libraries w/internet use policy	Lead	93%

Targets

The sixth column displays the targets. Formatting here is unlimited; you have a choice of how many columns you want to display your targets. These can be short-term (one year or less) and/or long-term (two to three years). DDL's targets are illustrated below:

Perspective	Strategic Objectives	Measures	Type	Actual	Target
Customer	Expand customer base	Registered borrowers as a percent of the service population	Lag	62%	98%
	Retain existing customers	Percent repeat program registrants	Lag	25%	60%
	Create value for customers	Number of promotional events	Lead	5	7
		Customer satisfaction rate	Lag	89%	100%

(Perspective)	(Strategic Objectives)	(Measures)	(Type)	(Actual)	(Target)
Internal Process	Optimize facilities	Facilities use rate	Lag	33%	85%
		Total collections per capita	Lag	2.5	3.1
	Improve resources	Average age of collection	Lead	6.25 yrs	4
	Enhance access	Number of training facilities	Lead	1	3
		Number of assistive technologies implemented	Lag	4	4
		Number of computer workstations/100 people	Lead	.04	1
Knowledge and Innovation	Recruit and retain qualified staff	Staff retention rate	Lag	98%	99%
	Develop required competencies	Percent of staff attending training	Lead	62%	75%
		Number of staff using scholarship program to obtain MLS	Lead	2	4
	Develop leadership & foster innovation	Number of programming best practice kits adopted	Lead	28	35
Financial	Encourage local investmetn	Total local operating income per capita	Lag	$20.28	$40
		Total local capital expenditures per capita	Lag	$.52	$1
	Streamline governance	Number of libraries in county systems	Lag	13	35
	Create developmental policies	Percent of libraries with collection development policy	Lead	87%	
		Percent of libraries w/internet use policy	Lead	93%	

Additional columns may be added to reflect owners of measures, initiatives, and the budget needed to implement them. An example can look like this:

Perspective	Strategic Objectives	Measures	Type	Actual	Target	Owner	Initiative	Budget
Customer	Expand customer base	Registered borrowers as a percent of the service population	Lag	62%	98%	LO	XX	XX
	Retain existing customers	Percent repeat program registrants	Lag	25%	60%	KG	XX	XX
	Create value for customers	Number of promotional events	Lead	5	7	AN	XX	XX
		Customer satisfaction rate	Lag	89%	100%	DW	XX	XX
Internal Process	Optimize facilities	Facilities use rate	Lag	33%	85%	JP	XX	XX
		Total collections per capita	Lag	2.5	3.1	SN	XX	XX
		Average age of collection	Lead	6.25 years	4	VA	XX	XX
	Enhance access	Number of training facilities	Lead	1	3	JP	XX	XX
		Number of assistive technologies implemented	Lead	4	4	JP	XX	XX
		Number of computer workstations/100 people	Lead	.04	1	JP	XX	XX

(Perspective)	(Strategic Objectives)	(Measures)	(Type)	(Actual)	(Target)	(Owner)	(Initiative)	(Budget)
Knowledge and Innovation	Recruit and retain qualified staff	Staff retention rate	Lag	98%	99%	SB	XX	XX
	Develop required competencies	Percent of staff attending training	Lead	62%	75%	LO	XX	XX
		Number of staff using MLS scholarship program	Lead	2	4	AN	XX	XX
	Develop leadership & foster innovation	Number of programming best practice kits adopted	Lead	28	35	PL	XX	XX
Financial	Encourage local investment	Total local operating income per capita	Lag	$20.28	$40	DW	XX	XX
	Streamline governance	Total local capital expenditures per capita	Lag	$.52	$1	DW	XX	XX
		Number of libraries county systems	Lag	13	35	AN	XX	XX
	Create developmetnal policies	Percent of libraries with collection development policy	Lead	87%	100%	JT	XX	XX
		Percent of libraries w/ internet use policy	Lead	93%	100%	JT	XX	XX

Comments

An optional last column can be added to reflect any comments concerning the reasons why the target goals are not being achieved during the planned time period. For example, why did we perform poorly in this quarter in the number of staff completing required training?

You can now see that when completed, the BSC can be a simple, one-page summary document which can be used and understood by every employee or manager who needs to see the big picture. The report highlights key objectives, measures, and performance that show where the organization is headed and the resources that are needed to reach its strategic goals.

However, it is important to remember that simply creating a BSC will not improve performance. It is a feedback system where managers assess the rate of progress towards the achievement of a strategy.

How Can a Balanced Scorecard Be Used?

A Balanced Scorecard can be used in many different ways. According to the research findings of Paul R. Niven, renowned author of the *Balanced Scorecard Step-by-Step: Maximizing Performance and Maintaining Results* (2002), a Balanced Scorecard can be used as a measurement system, a strategic management system, and a communication tool. It is

- a measurement system because it monitors lead and lag measures within each Perspective. The drivers of this measurement system are the organization's vision and strategy rather than the traditional financial controls.
- a strategic management system because it allows the alignment of performance measures with the organization's strategy. No longer are measures collected "just in case we need them," or because "we have always been collecting these measures" but because the data that are collected support strategy and key objectives.
- a communication tool because it illustrates, in one place, the interdependent components that make up the entire organization's strategy and the goals that it aims to achieve through carefully crafted measures designed to monitor progress. At the Delaware Divisions of Libraries (DDL), employees' performance plans are aligned with their individual scorecards. This clarifies to the employees the specific roles they play in advancing the division's strategy. Clearly understanding the organization's strategy, where they fit, and where the organization is heading unleashes hidden talents and empowers employees to be innovative and creative.

12

A Closer Look
at the Perspectives

*"Learning is not attained by chance, it must be sought for with ardor
and attended to with diligence."*
— Abigail Adams
(1744–1818)

Customer Perspective

This Perspective could very well be the most important one of all, only because everything an organization does is done to ultimately benefit customers. Customers are the top judges when it comes to defining their likes, dislikes, preferences and other satisfaction requirements. Organizations would cease to exist and their progress could not be sustained without satisfied and loyal customers.

Metaphorically, this Perspective can be seen as the magnifying glass of all the Perspectives. Everything you do should always focus on the customer. Focus not only on the external things that the customer can see, feel, and experience, like programming, reference, and building environment, but also on things that are invisible to the customer, like internal processes that make the external possible, such as products and services provided by libraries (i.e., this is the cause and effect link between the Customer and the Internal Processes perspectives). Ask yourself the following questions: "If I were the customer, what are the attributes I would be looking for? What would I consider convenient, but high quality? How would I want to be treated? What are the things that would create value for me and make me want to come back?"

It would seem easy to tackle this Perspective, but it can be very complicated especially for a service entity like a library. Libraries, all too often, fall into the trap of "being all things to everybody." Indeed, it may seem like this is the case all the time. This lack of focus however, contributes to broad, unfocused efforts and perpetuates frustration.

Customer Segmentation

Just like there are layers of skin in an onion, similarly there are layers of customers within the a demographic group (see Table 12.1— Results of the Dover Public Library study). A successful organization's infrastructure, resources, efforts and strategy must support the needs of each layer.

Defining who your target customers are, identifying what they value, determining their requirements and preferences, and systematically measuring their levels of satisfaction with your services lay the foundation for the whole strategic plan. These details also serve as guidelines when developing the remaining perspectives within the scorecard.

Marshal Cohen, in *Why Customers Do What They Do*, describes the challenges posed by today's customers:

> Consumers today are much more complex than ever before. First, purchases often range across a very wide range of products so that the lifestyle of choice (adventure-loving, family of four, for instance) can be achieved. Second, there are the dynamics that individuals today must endure at every level, whether national, personal, or workplace-related. We live in a world of contradictions, and professionals need to incorporate that point in their product messages. If your brand can communicate this understanding, it will prove to consumers that your brand and your company relate to their complex lifestyles [p. 35].

A small pilot study conducted in one very busy library in Dover, Delaware, proved to be an eye-opener in reference to customer segmentation. Customer segmentation by customer interests (target marketing) is second nature to private industry, but public sector organizations do not usually go beyond census data. Traditionally, we conduct customer segmentation using demographics. This study, however, revealed that not all individuals in the "young adult" group and other groups segmented by age had the same motivators for visiting a library. The findings indicate that segmentation by grouping customers with similar interests and motivators for visiting a library was a more effective way of determining what the customers valued.

A qualitative content analysis of responses was used to generate eight basic reasons for library attendance, plus an "Other" category (see Table 12.1). These eight identity-related reasons were then used to develop motivation categories.

This is an example of a study that helps provide cause and effect data to the rest of the BSC perspectives. To elaborate, objectives and measures in the Internal Processes perspective focus on developing programs targeted to the various customer "bundles" or motivational categories. For the Learning and Growth perspective, employees would have to receive training or additional information on how to develop and deploy such programs. Finally, for the Financial Perspective, we would be looking for a

---

Table 12.1
Delaware Public Libraries
Customer Segmentation Study

Explorers: Users who are simply curious and love to learn new things, but do not have an agenda driving their visits. They know that they will find something interesting at the library.

Facilitators: Users who are there largely to support someone else. They come to cultivate library-going and behavior in their children, or because they want to check out audio books for a friend.

Scholars: Users who have a deep interest and a history of research work in one topic area. Examples of users in this category are those who describe themselves as a "genealogist" or a "religious scholar." These individuals often use the interlibrary loan services or travel to specific libraries with supportive collections.

Problem Solvers: Users who have a specific question or problem that they're trying to solve. This includes users planning a trip, learning about a new pregnancy, or looking for information on how to write a job resume.

Hobbyists: Users who have a specific interest area, and visit the library to further that particular interest. Interesting examples include the NASCAR specialist and the Aviation buff, both of whom visit the library to stay on top of what is new in their field.

Experience Seekers: Users who perceive the library as a venue for entertainment or social connection. They come to the library to be around people, particularly people like themselves, or to read the newspaper. They may also come to check out books or DVDs, but are less concerned about the books or DVDs they choose, and really describe themselves as looking for something to occupy their time.

Patrons: Users who have a strong sense of belonging to the library, and join the local library immediately when they change communities. They often volunteer for the library, and go out of their way to bring other, less committed users with them.

Spiritual Pilgrims: Users who focus on the library as a place of reflection or rejuvenation. They speak of the library as their "peace" place, or as a "constant" in their life. They come to the library because it nurtures a spiritual need.

Others: This category includes a range of users whose motivations do not fall into any of the above categories. Examples include users who are at the library just to drop something off or pick something up, or the individual that has to prove he is at the library in order to get credit for another program. Table 2 summarizes how the 113 library users are distributed across these nine categories.

---

greater return on investment because the appropriated funds would — ideally — be expended more effectively. The assumption that if you provide a program, patrons will come, does not always hold true. The program must be related to their interests.

Prior to the customer segmentation study, the Division of Libraries had to clearly identify the methods it employs to understand customer requirements, expectations, and preferences (listening and learning methods). The agency also had to identify methods by customer groups in order to complete the Baldrige quality application (See Table 12.1). It is important to build relationships with your customers so that you can effectively listen and learn from them (see Customer Relationship building in Table 12.2).

Once organizations have identified customers' requirements and preferences and have "won their business," they have to make sure that they keep the customers happy. Building and maintaining good relationships with customers is a continuous process that requires a well-developed strategy not only in acquiring them but also earning their loyalty and satisfaction (tables 12.3 and 12.4). An example is the way DDL contracts with private sector performers to perform at the Summer Library Reading Programs. The process for selecting the performer and the subsequent relationship between the organization and the performer affects the quality delivered to the customer. The focus here is to develop process measures that will ensure successful outcomes (cause and effect link to the next perspective which is Internal Processes).

Table 12.2
Types of Listening and Learning Methods
to Build Customer Relationships

Segment	Listening/Learning Method	Frequency
Public Libraries and the Library Community in General and Stakeholders Town Meetings	• Town meetings • Surveys • Research • Focus groups • Automation services meetings • Technology (examples: integrated library system; virtual reference) • Statewide Master Plan • Communication methods (Fig. P.1–2)	BA A, AH A, AH A, AH A, AH M D M, D, A, B, A A A, BA, D, M, Q, W
General Public	• Media • Surveys • Focus groups • Advisory council mtgs. • Outreach efforts	D, W, Q, A A, M A, AH BA A, H

(Segment)	(Listening/Learning Method)	(Frequency)
Employees	• Staff meetings	M, Q, A
	• One-on-one meetings	W
	• Surveys	A, AH
	• Communication methods (Fig. P.1–2)	A, BaA, D, M, Q, W
Legend: A=annually, AH=ad hoc, BA=bi-annually, D=daily, M=monthly, Q=quarterly, W=weekly		

Table 12.3
Customer Relationship Cycle and Approach

Customer Relationship Cycle	*DDL Approach*
Attract	• Collaborate with various types of libraries to promote different events • Partner with instructors and organizations who provide computer and performance improvement training to the public library staff community • Collaborate with the Bill and Melinda Gates Foundation to provide computers and training to libraries • Obtain funding from state and other sources • Provide remote library services at public events hosted by businesses or state agencies • Determine through needs assessments and surveys what satisfies current users and what needs to be done to attract non-users • Provide innovative, user-friendly technology with download capabilities • Collect, analyze and report results indicating stewardship of tax dollars and return on investment
Maintain	• Provide professional, courteous, and timely customer service • Establish Best Practice manuals for programming • Embed DDL's values in all planning and activities (Service, Access, Excellence) • Maintain a formal complaint process

Follow-up	• Ensure that the two-way communication methods remain open and functional • Follow up to ensure customer's complaint has been resolved in a satisfactory manner • Provide surveys and evaluation forms at programming events to ensure customer expectations were met, and determine how they can be met or exceeded in future events
Set-Up	• Set up systems that provide and support multiple and multi-type means of access to information that is current, accurate, and timely • Conduct demographic analysis to determine current and upcoming trends

Table 12.4
Customer Relationship Requirements

Relationship Requirements:

    - Fair treatment [PL, GP, KS, E]

    -Interested, accessible, and cooperative leaders, and staff [PL, GP, KS, E]

    -Welcoming environment [PL, GP, KS, E]

    -Good Communication [PL, GP, KS, E]

    -Opportunity to get involved [PL, KS, E]

Contact Requirements:

    -Ease of access [PL, GP, KS, E]

    -Responsiveness [PL, GP, KS, E]

    -Competent employee [PL, GP, KS, E]

    -Accurate information [PL, GP, KS, E]

PL=public libraries, GP-general public, KS=key stakeholders, E=employees

Internal vs. External Customers

In library lingo, a customer is usually referred to as a patron. In broad terms, customers are segmented into two groups: external and internal. Patrons are considered external customers, but so are other agencies, other libraries, legislators, and private industry vendors (suppliers). Internal customers are mainly the employees.

Cause and Effect Linkages to the Customer Perspective

STRATEGIC PLANNING

Current and future customer preferences and requirements, and other input information related to the business environment, define the direction of the strategic plan as well as the design of the process that create value for the customer. Having this information also guides leadership in setting the direction or the vision for the organization.

KNOWLEDGE MANAGEMENT AND GROWTH

The management and dissemination of knowledge gleaned from various sources, such as customer complaint data, service and product trends, market data, benchmarking, satisfaction data, employee satisfaction findings and professional development, validates customer requirements and are used to define customer-related results.

FINANCIAL

Targeted value creation processes and services, streamlined internal operations, targeted decision-making measures all contribute to a greater return on investment and wiser use of all resources.

Internal Processes Perspective

The key question we have to address in this perspective is "What internal processes can we streamline or do we have to excel at in order to satisfy our stakeholders and customers?"

This question forces us to examine what we are currently doing or not doing, and how this affects the value of our services to our stakeholders and customers. In extreme situations, it may mean the implementation of entirely new processes instead of incrementally trying to improve current processes that are ineffective. A useful tool to help employees see the sequential steps in a process that needs to be modified is a flowchart or a process flow diagram. It does not have to be elaborate or require any special software or skills. It can be a hand-drawn diagram showing the progression of steps from the beginning to the end of a process. The completed process flow diagram allows employees and managers to look at problem areas, identify redundancies, and eliminate steps that are unnecessary. At times, processes are streamlined by eliminating duplicative steps or combining steps, thus shortening the length of the process. Figure 12.1 is an example of a process flow diagram or flowchart:

A good tool to use to identify process bottlenecks is the workflow chart. A workflow chart is a spatial illustration of how information, goods, or people move in a process. Figure 12.2 illustrates the workflow process of paying a vendor through the state system. Right from the beginning, we can see where a bottleneck occurs. Accounting receives the invoices which are distributed to the appropriate administrators for their review and approval to proceed with payment. The administrators send the invoices back to accounting. Accounting then proceeds to send the invoices to the staff accountant. To save time, the administrators can send their invoices straight to the staff accountant (dotted line) instead of re-directing them back to the accounting office.

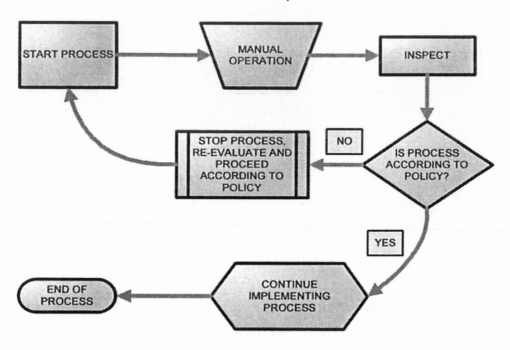

Figure 12.1 Sample of a Flowchart.

What does this process have to do with related measures in the scorecard? One of the measures might relate to the cycle time of processing payments. Of course, the cycle time will be significantly reduced if the process is streamlined.

Process management is a continuous improvement journey that changes and evolves as customer needs and wants change. High performing organizations identify and continuously improve both their key business and support processes.

In any organization, there is always a "subject matter expert" or a "process owner" who is intimately involved in managing a specific process. However, process improvement is a collective responsibility, and should not remain within the purview of the process owner or the subject matter expert only.

The measures that should be collected in this perspective depends on what is strategically critical to your operations that create a valuable relationship with the customer.

Key Business vs. Support Processes

The Baldrige Criteria classify processes into two broad categories. The first focuses on the processes that create value for the customer (mission-oriented or value-creation processes) and the second focuses on the support processes that make the value creation processes possible (see Figure 12.4). For example, a process that creates value for the customer may be the provision and availability of PCs connected to the Internet.

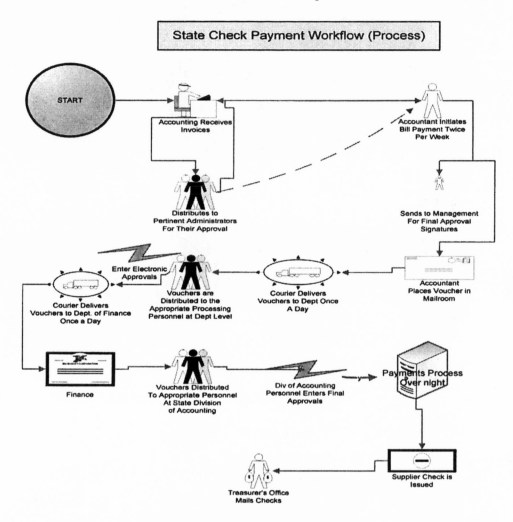

Figure 12.2 *Sample Workflow Diagram.*

A support process that may go hand in hand with this is the troubleshooting and maintenance function provided by the IT division. Figure 12.3 illustrates how the key business processes can be segmented by Balanced Scorecard (BSC) Perspectives.

Cause and Effect Linkages to Value Creation and Support Processes

SENIOR LEADERSHIP AND THE GOVERNANCE SYSTEM

Senior leaders must understand and ensure that key business processes are essential to the growth and success of the organization and that they must be designed to

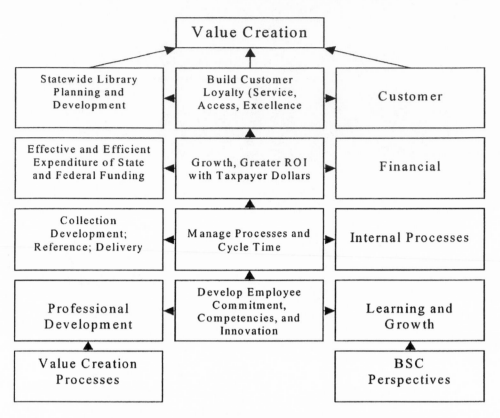

Figure 12.3 Key Business Processes by BSC Perspective.

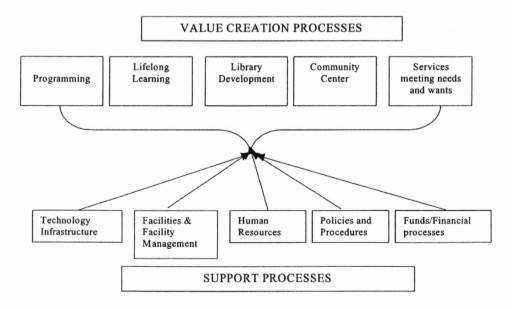

Figure 12.4 Relationship between Support and Value Creation Processes.

consistently support and promote the organization's strategic objectives and public responsibilities.

Customer Requirements, Preferences,
Complaints, and Satisfaction

These are critical for everyone to understand as a platform for designing processes that create value for the customer.

Knowledge Management and Growth

Better benchmarking helps with improved and more targeted key business processes. In addition, flexible work systems, staff training, and recognition are essential in recognizing and identifying key business processes. They help define requirements and set priorities for support processes.

Financial

Optimum operational efficiency, more knowledgeable staff, efficient and effective value creation processes, and a commitment to continuous improvement are critical factors that ensure continued financial support from satisfied customers and informed stakeholders. The more valuable an organization is, the more sustainable it becomes.

Knowledge and Growth Perspective

The key question for this perspective is "To achieve our vision, how will we sustain our ability to change and improve?" This perspective addresses not only employee learning and development but also the work environment, work systems, and the organizational culture. Over the year, we've moved from the industrial age worker to the information age worker, and, now, to the knowledge worker. Contrary to some beliefs, the knowledge bank of any organization is not technology, but its people. While an organization must keep up with technology to maintain a competitive edge, the knowledge bank is of no use if it's fed the wrong information. In a climate of rapid technological change, people must be in a continuous learning mode. Ongoing training of competent workers and the application of what is learned drive continuous improvement and innovation. The Baldrige Criteria emphasize that there should be a synergy between technology and people to make information available throughout all levels of an organization. Information vital to decision making should be readily available to everyone that needs it. Baldrige calls it "high performance work systems."

Government agencies often find themselves unable to compete with industry

167

because they can't keep up with the pay scales of technical workers. In addition, when faced with budget cuts, unfortunately, the staff training budget is one of the first to be trimmed or eliminated. Training is a leading indicator that can be tracked and, when improved, can be a predictor of future success. This measure can guide managers in directing training funds where they can help the most.

A majority of baby boomers will be retiring within the next three to five years. Arlene Dohm, an economist in the Office of Employment Projections, Bureau of Labor, reported in "Gauging the Labor Force Effects of Retiring Baby Boomers" that 56.5 percent of the national librarian workforce in 1998 was over the age of 45. Given the projected trend, by 2008, more than half of the librarian workforce will have retired.

For this reason it is urgent that libraries work on transferring knowledge and engaging in succession planning. Establishing and sustaining operational and system-wide performance excellence through the use of the Baldrige Criteria and the Balanced Scorecard will assist libraries in transferring knowledge to the future generations of librarians.

The Knowledge and Learning Perspective also helps promote employee satisfaction, safety, and well-being. It covers motivation, ergonomics, organizational climate, and the employee reward and recognition system. Just as a healthy body lives longer, so does a high-performing organization. A competent, satisfied and loyal workforce allows an organization to thrive and to succeed. The Baldrige Criteria that address the Learning and Growth Perspective are categories 4 (Knowledge Management) and 5 (Human Resource Focus).

Cause and Effect Linkages to the Learning and Growth Perspective

CUSTOMER

Improved processes due to the effective use of internal and external information and employee learning and empowerment lead to improved products and services for customers, and are therefore a good predictor of customer satisfaction and loyalty.

INTERNAL PROCESSES

Skilled, creative, and satisfied employees question current work systems and are empowered to improve old or create new internal processes; therefore, this is a good predictor of value-creating services for customers.

FINANCIAL

Satisfied and loyal customers lead to increased and sustained revenues.

The Financial Perspective

The key question to this perspective is "To succeed financially, how should we appear to our stakeholders?" When Kaplan and Norton originally designed the Balanced Scorecard, their intent was not to eliminate the financial measurement piece but to balance it because so many organizations were focused on that perspective alone when measuring their success. Many public organizations place the Knowledge and Growth Perspective, which is the human resources piece, at the bottom as a way of emphasizing that the foundation of an organization is its employees. The Delaware Division of Libraries believes its employees are its foundation, but also realizes that without funding, nothing can happen, even with the most outstanding employees. Funding supports the division's initiatives, training and development, and employee well-being (Knowledge and Growth perspective), which in turn enables the planning and design of efficient and effective processes (Internal Processes Perspective), which in turn allows for the effective delivery of quality products and services to its customers, which ought to promote customer satisfaction and loyalty (Customer Perspective). The satisfied and loyal customer will then be more likely to support additional funding (Financial Perspective), and the cycle continues. So what is really happening here? Note that every time the cycle starts up again, the financial processes have been improved and have become more efficient. When funds are allocated and spent more wisely, the return on investment increases proportionately. The goal of the Financial Perspective for public entities is not to get more money for the sake of having additional funds, but to improve the return on investment. After all, we are stewards of taxpayers' money.

Libraries have been collecting a lot of financial data, especially on a per capita basis (National Center for Education Statistics library ranking data). However, these per capita measures are generally not associated or aligned with any overall national strategic direction.

Currently, these national data are being used to rank states, but there may be a fallacy to this ranking. What is good and works well for Texas may not work in New York, and so on. These financial measures must be looked at from a strategic point of view and be translated and linked to the individual agency's objectives and goals, and socio-economic environment.

To illustrate this further, in the most recent FSCS statistics from 2003 — the latest published by NCES as of the date of this writing — Delaware ranks eighth in the nation in per capita income. Currently, DDL receives $3.8 million in state funds to distribute to public libraries. Per capita that amount is $3.21. As DDL's vision states, if we want to be "first in the nation," a spot which is currently held by the state of Ohio, we have to distribute $33.7 million at $40 per capita. Is this realistic for Delaware? It can't happen under the current economic and market situation. Other strategic questions that need to be addressed are: If we increase the per capita state income, will that discourage the already low local investment? What goals can we set to find a happy medium? This is the kind of analysis a Balanced Scorecard would encourage because the measures that you select will be directly linked to your particular objective or goal.

Cause and Effect Linkages to the Financial Perspective

CUSTOMER

Financial and market results are used to understand the requirements and preferences of customers and the market in general. These results help with the strategic planning process, priority setting, and analysis.

KNOWLEDGE AND GROWTH

Financial results can be linked to the effectiveness of employee training, employee motivation and well-being. Reverse this statement and it also holds true: Effective training, employee well-being and motivation contribute to improved financial performance.

INTERNAL PROCESSES

Key business and support processes enhance financial and market results. Processes can be improved continuously by investing in ongoing learning and development aligned with individual and organizational needs.

13

Developing and Deploying
Your Balanced Scorecard

*"We learn by example and by direct experience because there are real
limits to the adequacy of verbal instruction. "*
— Malcolm Gladwell

The time has come to roll up your sleeves for a discussion of how to start developing and deploying the first draft of a Balanced Scorecard. Typically, a BSC is developed by the collective work of several teams as seen in Figure 13.1. The first team is the executive team, which includes managers who directly oversee a department or a division. Their responsibilities are to chart the direction of their units, which they do by developing individual strategy maps. They identify objectives (what needs to be done) and targets (the expected degree of improvement). The targets are important because they are the determinants of the amount of funding the executive team is willing to commit to achieve the goals and objectives. The members of the executive team are also responsible for "championing" the BSC and keeping the two-way communication channels open and clear to ensure everyone at all levels understand each development and deployment stage. It is also the responsibility of the executive team to determine the composition of the next team, which is the implementation team. The implementation team is responsible for carrying the scorecard to its completion. This team rounds out the Balanced Scorecard by developing and defining measures, targets, budgets, and initiatives. They determine the best methods of distilling, collecting and analyzing data, and facilitate the cascading of multiple scorecards. They too must communicate clearly an openly with the staff.

Within the implementation team there is a team leader or a project manager. This person is responsible for the success of the scorecard. He or she should be someone who views the scorecard as a critical project and one that is vital to the success of the organization. This person keeps the team focused and on track, communicates progress to all stakeholders, and ensures open two-way communication between the executive and implementation teams.

In organizations where BSC knowledge and experience are at the beginning stages, a fourth team is usually needed to provide technical advice and assistance. This team is often just one person, an external consultant who is first and foremost a BSC expert. An ideal facilitator is one who also possesses strong communication and instructional skills. The facilitator assists with the recommendation of measures and tools that will help in the collection and organization of scorecard measures and also takes the lead in responding to technical questions.

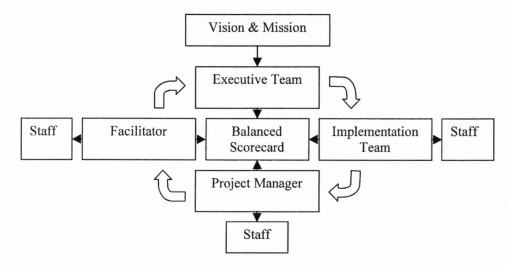

Figure 13.1 Balanced Scorecard Teams.

We realize that the massive involvement of people and resources with this project may not be possible for many libraries, but the extent and comprehensiveness of the project can be trimmed down to basics. In small agencies, all the tasks can be accomplished by a small team and maintained by a single person.

At the Delaware Division of Libraries, the executive team is a one-person team, the director; the implementation team consists of one person who serves as the project leader; and the facilitators are the Balanced Scorecard consultants who developed the BSC software our agency is using. Owners of measures are the administrative librarians who are accountable for overseeing the measures related to their areas of responsibility.

The BSC is a useful tool in demonstrating to employees how their jobs are connected with the organization's goals and how they are accountable for achieving certain objectives. By assigning accountability throughout all levels of the organization, the scorecard gives meaning to staff performance plans and evaluations. This is especially important to public sector entities, where accountability and responsibility are often diffused and unclear.

Development Steps

The big picture implementation steps — C.A.R.D., as developed by Ralph Smith, vice president of Strategic Services for the Orion Development Group — are seen in Table 13.1. Each step will be discussed separately in the paragraphs that follow.

Table 13.1 C.A.R.D. Implementation Steps		
Steps	*From*	*To (Product)*
Chart strategic direction	**Mission and vision identified**	**Strategic themes (Priorities) identified through strategy map**
Analysis	**Strategy map**	**First draft scorecard**
Revision	**First draft scorecard**	**Completed Balanced Scorecard**
Deployment	**Completed scorecard**	**System-wide implementation**

Source: Adapted from Orion Development Group, 2005.

Chart Strategic Direction

This "C" phase is usually the responsibility of the executive team. It focuses on the following steps:

- Identify appropriate organizational unit for BSC
- Create and reviewing mission and vision statements
- Define strategic objectives that support mission and vision
- Determine whether sufficient cause-and-effect linkages exist
- Hand off objectives to implementation team

IDENTIFY APPROPRIATE ORGANIZATIONAL
UNIT FOR THE BALANCED SCORECARD

A BSC does not always have to be developed for an entire organization. This is especially true of a large and diverse organization because it could be difficult to find a manageable number of relevant measures. It may be easier to start with discrete departments or divisions that have similar or related functions.

CREATE OR REVIEW MISSION AND VISION STATEMENTS

There are senior leaders who, when independently asked what the vision and mission of their organization are, come up with different answers and ideas as to why their organization exists or what its future direction may be. It is absolutely imperative that the leadership team be on the same page when it comes to mission and vision. Otherwise, it will be difficult to communicate a "confusion of voices" to the rest of the workforce, and employees will not know how they fit in the big blurry picture.

The Balanced Scorecard translates the mission, vision, and strategies into performance objectives and measures in each of the scorecard perspectives. Decoding the organizational "DNA" allows the employees to understand how their jobs are aligned with achieving the mission and vision of their organization. The BSC serves as a map to guide both leaders and employees in achieving the organization's mission and vision.

WHAT IS A MISSION STATEMENT?

A mission statement explains your reason for existence — your core purpose. It answers the question "What is this organization's fundamental purpose?" The mission needs to be clearly communicated to its employees, customers and stakeholders.

CHARACTERISTICS OF A GOOD MISSION STATEMENT

- *Simple and clear:* Broad statements of value or goodness do not make good mission statements because they are not clear enough to allow employees to focus their energies on achieving the mission. A good example of a clear and simple message is Wal-Mart's mission statement: *"To give ordinary folks the chance to buy the same things as rich people."*
- *Easy to understand and communicate*: Your mission should be written in plain language easily understood by all. Avoid buzzwords or jargon. *"To make people happy."*
- *Long term in nature:* Mission statements should be written to serve as a lasting guide to action and decisions. They should remain relevant for a long time. The IRS: *"To provide America's taxpayers with top-quality service by helping them understand and meet their tax responsibilities by applying the tax law with integrity and fairness to all."*
- *Customer-focused:* Define your mission in terms of who you serve, your customers, rather than the services you provide or what you produce. American Insttute of Certified Public Accountants: *"[To] provide members with the resources, information, and leadership that enable them to provide valuable*

services in the highest professional manner to benefit the public as well as employees and clients."

What is a vision statement? A vision statement expresses a realistic, credible, and attractive future for your organization. It provides a picture of what the organization intends to be, say, three, five, or ten years in the future.

CHARACTERISTICS OF A GOOD VISION STATEMENT

- *Concise:* The best vision statements are those that grab your attention and immediately draw you in without boring you with pages of mundane and meaningless rhetoric.

    President Kennedy, May 25, 1961: *"I believe that this nation should commit itself to achieving, before this decade is out, of landing a man on the Moon, and returning him safely to the Earth."*

- *Verifiable:* Can you provide evidence that you have achieved your vision? Is it verifiable? How many within your organization will be able to determine exactly when you become "world-class" or "leading edge"?

- *Clear and compelling:* people "get it" right away.

- Dr. Martin Luther King, Jr., August 28, 1963: *"I have a dream that one day on the red hills of Georgia that sons of former slaves and the sons of former slave owners will be able to sit down together at a table of brotherhood."*

DEFINE STRATEGIC OBJECTIVES
THAT SUPPORT MISSION AND VISION

Obstacles are those frightful things you see when you take yours eyes off your goal.

— Henry Ford

As defined earlier, a mission is "what you do and why you are in business," while a vision is "how you envision your organization to look like in the future," and the strategic plan is your road map of how to get there.

"Strategos" in Greek means the leader of a group, particularly in the military. The strategos is the person who lays out the strategy for how to win the war. Keep the strategic planning process and the plan itself easy to understand. Prioritize the strategic goals and objectives, define roles and responsibilities, and make sure all initiatives support the organization's priorities.

Whether your organization has a strategic plan or not, a good exercise to do is the SWOT analysis to start determining what the organization's true objectives should be. A common technique is to write down your organizational strengths, weaknesses, opportunities and threats on separate sticky notes. Then, sort each sticky note by the four Balanced Scorecard perspectives. Place those that have to do with people, training and internal communications in the Learning and Growth perspective; those that have to do with processes, products, cycle times in the Internal Processes perspective; those that have to do with external issues, customers, stakeholders, competitors, market, in the Customer perspective; and those that have to do with money issues in the Financial perspective. After completing this exercise, it would be interesting to review and compare your findings with your established federal LSTA plan. It would not be surprising to discover that certain things were not addressed or anticipated in the plan.

It is critical that every objective has a strategic measure associated with it. In the previous performance objective example—"Retain existing customers"—a measure might be "Retention rate of active borrowers." This would be calculated by dividing what you would define as an active borrower by the total number of cardholders (sum of active and inactive). This allows you to monitor progress and assess effectiveness in every phase of the strategic plan. After all, it is not only important to make sure you monitor your weaknesses and challenges, but to make sure you sustain your strengths.

DETERMINE WHETHER SUFFICIENT CAUSE AND EFFECT LINKAGES EXIST

This is critical step where the scorecard comes together and starts to develop meaning. The cause and effect linkages among the performance objectives makes it easier for users to understand the organization's strategy and share it with others. This is the phase where the development of a well-constructed strategy map is initiated, with limited number of precise objectives that define the primary drivers of overall agency success.

In continuing with the "sticky note" exercise, you would now look at each perspective separately. For example, in the Financial perspective, determine which sticky note speaks to the top financial objective. Then you would ask yourself, "What other financial objectives would cause the top one to happen?" Place all responses that meet this criterion under the top financial objective and draw connecting arrows under each one. At this point there may be financial objectives that do not fit anywhere or you may determine that additional objectives are needed to achieve the top one. For those that do not fit under the classification under consideration, ask yourself why. Either it is not related to your top objective and if so, get rid of it, or if this is not the case, supporting objectives may be needed to complete your strategy. Follow this process until all perspectives are complete and until all objectives are connected. The Delaware Division of Libraries strategy map (Figure 13.2) is shown below. Figure 13.3 illustrates the cause and effect relationship among all four perspectives.

Linking the objectives with cause and effect arrows is also an exercise in pri-

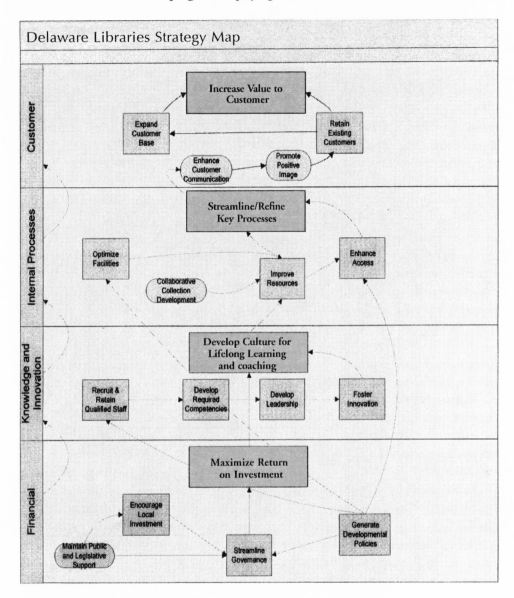

Figure 13.2 *Delaware Libraries Strategy Map. Delaware Division of Libraries' Strategy Map Using All Four Balanced Scorecard Perspective.*

oritization. In order to achieve your mission or your number one goal, you must decide which objective must come first before you can accomplish the one above it. In the public sector, the Customer Perspective is elevated to the top and greater emphasis is placed on accountability and results to meet citizen requirements and preferences. Think of it as building a house. First comes the foundation, then the

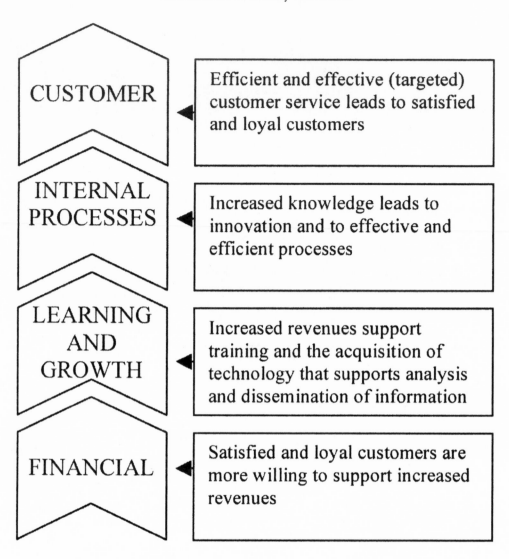

Figure 13.3 Cause and Effect Relationships Between Perspectives.

frame, then the electrical wiring, then the sheetrock, and so on, until you end up with the house. If any one of these objectives are skipped or not appropriately identified and aligned, then the structural integrity of the house is compromised.

A strategy map is a two-dimensional figure as shown in Figure 13.4. Horizontally, it illustrates the alignment between mission, vision, strategy, measures, targets, budget, and initiatives. Vertically, it illustrates prioritization through the cause and effect linkages of the objectives.

Another useful tool to use when establishing cause and effect relationships is the

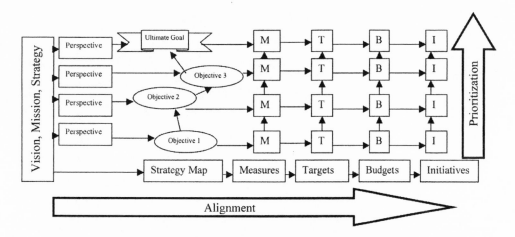

Figure 13.4 The Two Dimensions of a Strategy Map.

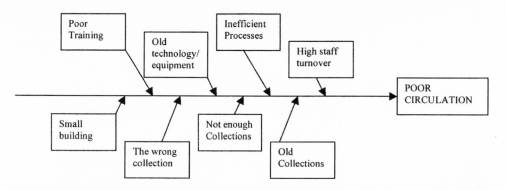

Figure 13.5 Fishbone Diagram Showing the Cause and Effect Relationship Between Poor Circulation and Related Measures.

fishbone diagram. You start by identifying either the problem or desired result first and then identifying the causes that are currently making something happen or the causes that will make your desired effect happen. With the fishbone diagram, all the pertinent causes are plotted along a causal line. These causes are in most cases the clues as to what kind of measures should be tracked for your organization to be successful. For example, after completing the SWOT analysis, if one of your Weaknesses is poor circulation of library materials, then you need to identify what negative causes may be responsible (Figure 13.5). If the desired result is to have high circulation, then these negative causes must be addressed (Figure 13.6). Of course, the measures would have to be prioritized, and the most urgent issues must be addressed first.

It is at this point that the executive team passes the Balanced Scorecard development baton to the implementation team. The senior executives define the mission,

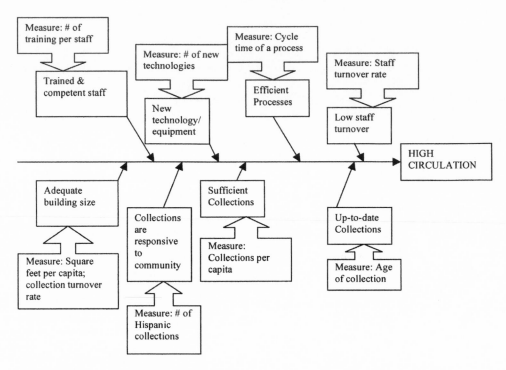

Figure 13.6 *Fishbone Diagram Showing the Cause and Effect Relationship Between High Circulation and Related Measures.*

vision and strategy to the implementation team and communicate the objectives and the logic behind their cause and effect relationships. Both teams must come to a consensus as to what these issues are. A useful communication tool that is used to document the objectives is an objectives information sheet such as the one displayed in Table 13.2. It saves time at this phase of development and ensures that everyone in the organization is on the same page. With this information, the implementation team now takes the lead and moves to the next phase of development.

Analysis

The "A" phase is usually the responsibility of the implementation team. It focuses on the following steps:

- Create first draft of desired measures
- Develop internal measurement expertise
- Determine availability of data
- Produce first scorecard
- Communicate back to the executives

Table 13.2
Objective Information Sheet

Objective: Expand Customer Base			
Short Name (for Map)	**Owner**	**Perspective**	**Status** (Draft, Final)
Expand Customer Base		Customer	Draft

Description (Describe this objective. It means.... It includes...)	
Strategic Theme (Which strategic theme(s) generated this objective?)	

Strategic Destination (What specific change are you working to achieve? "From what" to "what?")	**From:** Current State	**To:** Desired State

Rationale (What makes this objective important?)	
Red Flags (What concerns or cautions do you have regarding this objective?)	
Cause & Effect Relationships (What other objectives are directly linked to this objective in cause/effect relationships?)	

Possible Measures (What are possible ways to measure the impact of this objective?)
Measure:
Measure:
Measure:

Possible Initiatives (What are possible programs, activities, projects or actions that could be taken to achieve results?)
Initiative:
Initiative:
Initiative:

General Comments

Updated by:	Date:

Source: Adopted from Insightformation, Inc.

CREATE FIRST DRAFT OF DESIRED MEASURES AND DEVELOP INTERNAL MEASUREMENT EXPERTISE

Not everything that can be counted counts and not everything that counts can be counted.

— Albert Einstein

181

This step can be the most challenging. It is difficult to distill the vital few meas-ures that represent an organization's comprehensive strategy. Everything is impor-tant and a natural reaction is to get as many measures in as possible, "just to make sure we have a complete package." However, this can be the Achilles' heel of the

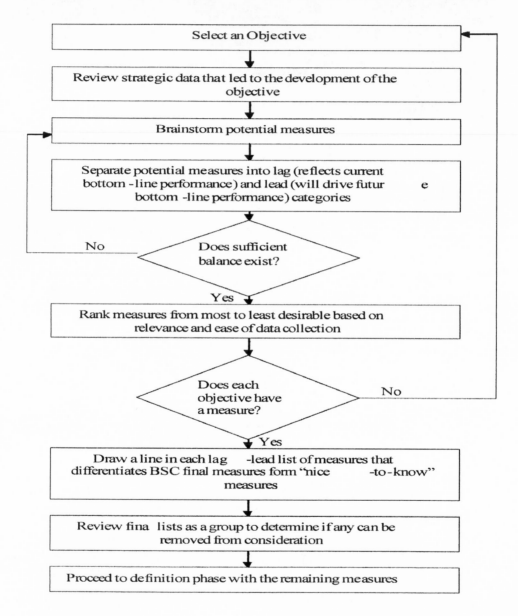

Figure 13.7 *Process for Developing First Draft Measures as Adopted by the Orion Devel-opment Group.*

Balanced Scorecard, and this is the trap libraries and many other entities all too often fall into.

After all the objectives have been selected, prioritized and defined, the next step is to assign meaningful measures to each that will help in the determination of progress.

Ideally, and according to many BSC experts, each BSC perspective should have between two and three objectives and each objective should have between two and three measures. This is especially important if the BSC is to be administered manually instead of automatically. A helpful flowchart (Figure 13.7), as developed by the Orion Development Group, summarizes the process of identifying the first draft measures.

Performance measures are indicators or standards used to assess performance against anticipated results or outcomes. They are typically quantitative and measurable, such as numbers, percentages, and dollars. Many times, these measures, if not defined, can have many different interpretations. Because communication is the name of the game, it is important to create a measure information sheet such as the one in Table 13.3 for every measure. This basically defines the measures, just like the executive team defined the objectives. This will facilitate communication and understanding of the measures used, the target numbers and the characteristics, purposes and methods of calculating the measures.

Data collection and analysis has typically been a challenging task for libraries. This is because the collection piece has been there, but not necessarily the analysis piece. All too often, libraries collect *data* to justify funding requests but they very seldom use *information,* the data readily available to them, to support decision making. It has been said that libraries are data rich but information poor. The focus must shift from "Are we doing it right?" to "Are we doing the right things to support and advance our core business?" This is what the analysis must reflect.

To develop meaningful performance measures, the organization must first know its core business and align these measures with the intended strategic outcomes. Contrary to popular belief, as we can see in the Figure 13.8 that follows, output measures are necessary, and lead to and support strategic outcomes.

Without a series of interconnected outputs, there cannot be outcomes. On the other hand, a common challenge with outcomes is that most are so far off in the future, or so global, that it takes a long time to achieve them. More often than not, the impact that various library programs might have on a community is unknown. For example, we cannot precisely measure the degree to which libraries play a role in the development of lifelong learning habits. There are other variables such as schools, families, society, internal motivation, and individual experiences that also play a vital role. These factors, however, should not be barriers to making lifelong

Table 13.3
Sample Measure Information Sheet

MEASURE INFORMATION SHEET: Measure Name

Short Name	Owner	Data Owner

Description:	
Data Source(s):	

Unit of Measure:		Update Frequency:	

Calculation:	
Update Process:	
Approval Process:	
Rationale:	
Concerns:	
Driving Initiative(s):	
Future Improvements:	

Drill Down Options	
Scorecard:	
Targeted:	
Ad Hoc BI:	
Future BI:	

Other Analysis Options	Links:	
	Other:	

Default Target:			
Polarity (direction):			

Default Threshold Band Values	Color	Lower Threshold Value	Upper Threshold Value
	Red		
	Yellow		
	Green		

Perspective	Objective

Source: Adopted from Insightformation, Inc.

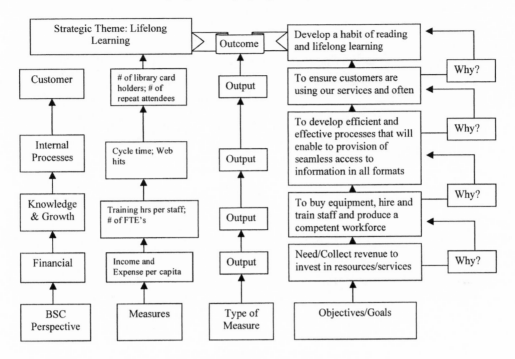

Figure 13.8 *Outputs to Outcomes.*

learning a strategic theme. Despite the fact that long term effectiveness is difficult to measure (especially with privacy issues and other mandates in the public sector), it is necessary to monitor short-term or intermediate outcomes to check if we are headed in the right direction. With time and practice, the process of selecting performance measures will get easier as they continue to be refined. Without ongoing and consistent monitoring, calibrating and documenting, the measures might become obsolete and irrelevant in relation to the achievement of the strategic goals.

Getting back to the core measures, the burning question is: "*What* do we measure? *Why, how* and *when* do we do measure it?" Figure 13.9 illustrates (reading from the bottom up and counterclockwise) the *why* and *how* components of developing performance measures.

The top rectangle in Fig. 13.9 is the ultimate outcome we intend to achieve. To develop the habit of reading and lifelong learning, the following sequential and cyclical process must take place first: collect revenue, hire and train competent staff, develop efficient and effective processes, and ensure customers are using your services.

The *what* component is driven by the goals and objectives and the *when* is determined by the organization's performance improvement plan. Through the Baldrige initiative, the Delaware Division of Libraries realized that collecting data

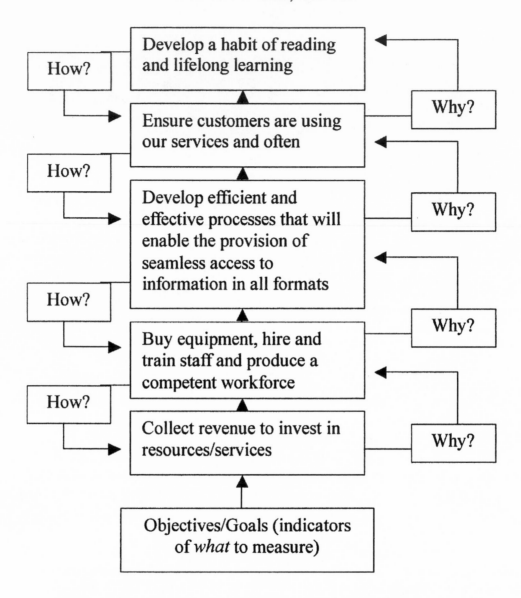

Figure 13.9 *Determining How to Develop Measures.*

once a year is not enough to make an impact on performance and is not frequent enough for effective and "just-in-time" decision making. Depending on the measure, data should be collected at least quarterly if not monthly. Major revenues, in the case of state and public libraries, or any other government agency, come once a year, so they cannot be measured monthly. On the other extreme, circulation can be monitored every 15 minutes if needed.

SOME BEST PRACTICE INFORMATION

According to research done by the National Partnership for Reinventing Government (*www.orau.gov*, August 1999), the "best practices" for balancing your mission and measures with customer, stakeholder, and employee perspectives include the following:

Establish a results-oriented set of measures that balance business, customer, and employee

- *Define what measures mean the most* to your employees, customers and stakeholders by (1) having them work and talk with each other, (2) creating familiar and easily understood body of measures, and (3) identifying clear measures that address their concerns.
- *Commit to initial change* by (1) leveraging expertise inside and outside the organization, (2) involving everyone (including the unions), (3) making consequences nonpunitive, (4) providing a clear and concise communication plan as to the establishment, monitoring, and reporting of measures.
- *Maintain flexibility* by (1) recognizing that performance management is a continual cycle, (2) limiting performance measures to the vital few, and (3) maintaining a balance between lag and lead measures (i.e., financial and nonfinancial).

Establish accountability at all levels of the organization

- *Lead by example.*
- *Cascade accountability* by (1) creating a culture of assessment, (2) assigning the responsibility for monitoring measures to all management and staff levels, and (3) involving all levels of stakeholders in performance management.
- *Keep the employee informed* via any form of communication desirable and available.
- *Keep the customer informed* via targeted communication channels (virtual and nonvirtual).
- *Make accountability work* by establishing and supporting an employee reward and recognition program.

Collect, use, and analyze data

- *Collect feedback data*, which can be obtained by enhancing customer access to your organization. The most familiar feedback form is a survey, which can be creatively designed and disseminated using various methods and formats.
- *Collect performance data* by (1) taking the time to ensure that the data are consistent and right, (2) ensuring that the data make sense and actually

mean something to the data users, (3) recognizing that data cannot at all times be all in one place (unless automated), and (4) centralizing data collection at the highest possible level (preferably automated).

• *Analyze data* by (1) combining feedback and performance data for a more complete and inclusive picture, (2) conducting root-cause analyses (i.e., fishbone cause and effect analysis), and (3) making sure the results of the analysis is visible and communicated to everyone.

Determine the Availability of Data

Hasn't everyone been in the position of knowing exactly what needs to be measured, but without current, systematic methods of collecting such measures? And then you have to wrestle with the politics and the bureaucratic rules that stifle creativity and implementation.

In any case, once all the measures have been identified and defined, you now have to determine the methods and systems used to collect the data. The most prominent reasons why it could be difficult to collect a needed data include the following:

• It may your first time collecting data. You have no baseline figures.
• The technological infrastructure is inadequate.
• Measures may not fit the BSC format.
• Data entry is asystematic and adhoc
• The measure's definition is too vague.

Generally, organizations collect and store data in a variety of places, programs and formats. Bill Barberg of Insightformation calls this the "data jungle." This disorganization is why it takes so long to compile a report or make a decision based on data.

The Balanced Scorecard provides an integrated framework for organizing and collecting needed data in one central place, which is why it is considered to be both an effective management and communication tool. It displays the selected measures in a dashboard format (once the implementation team has hacked through the data jungle), where executives and managers (or anyone in the organization, for that matter) can instantly see the rate of progression — not only for the measure, but the whole strategy. An automated BSC can be programmed to pull pertinent data from the data jungle so that as activities take place, the numbers and trend lines in the scorecard are updated on a predictable basis.

Produce First Scorecard and Communicate Back to the Executives

Now that all the data have been gathered and defined, it is time to put the first draft scorecard together. It is at this point where the implementation team assesses what it has gathered and decides on the "final cut" of measures, the time intervals they will be collected (i.e., monthly, quarterly, annually, etc.), and the format by which they will be displayed (i.e., trend or bar charts, color schemes, etc.). BSC experts recommend collecting data quarterly and annually but again, the interval depends on the number of measures and the organization's resources dedicated to updating the scorecard. The shorter the interval, the greater the need for additional resources because monitoring of measures is done on a more frequent basis. This first draft is what the implementation team takes back to the executives for review.

Revision

The "R" phase involves the active participation of the executive team in the implementation process. It focuses on the following steps:

- Revise categories
- Plan for collection of missing data
- Set targets

REVISE CATEGORIES

This is usually the feedback phase of the executive team to the implementation team after it has presented its first draft scorecard. Because the executive team is the ultimate group that is accountable for the organization, they would want the draft in a format that is easy to understand and also in a simplified format so that it can be easily interpreted. During this phase, it not uncommon for measures to be dropped, columns to be deleted or perspectives to be renamed.

PLAN FOR COLLECTION OF MISSING DATA

After going through the Baldrige assessment and the first three steps of developing a scorecard, measures that have not been collected before might be identified and added. Just because a measure has not been collected before does not mean that it should not go on the scorecard. Just the opposite. This shows that careful consideration and discussion among the team members has taken place and that they have attempted to identify what they need to track to be successful. Several points need to be considered when adopting new measures. One is the determination of how new measures will be collected. This may include the use of a new data collection tool, training of relevant staff, acquiring new technology, or establishing new processes. Another may simply be redefining already existing measures so that they are easier to understand and collect.

SET TARGETS

Measures are meaningless unless they have targets and comparison data. Further in this discussion about targets (Figure 13.10), we believe that through the use of benchmarking and variance analysis you can determine the degree by which the negative causal factors are preventing you from performing better and how you should address them. This is easier said than done. What will be the benefit of benchmarking if you do not first know the operating levels of your current processes (baseline measures)? Variance analysis will help determine those baselines. How DDL implemented this simple statistical process is discussed on page xxx. Figure 13.10 illustrates the prioritization cycle of target setting.

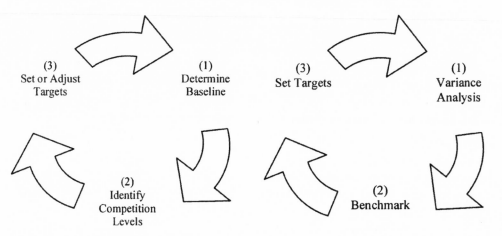

Figure 13.10 Prioritization Cycle of Target Setting.

The first step is to determine your baseline measures (internal). The DDL used variance analysis to do this, but your organization may use other methods as desired. The second step is to identify competition levels or to get the "pulse" of peers (external). How are they doing compared to you? Who is the best in the business and why? Once these questions are answered, the targets can be set or adjusted accordingly.

The DDL's experience has been that is it difficult to set targets based on benchmarking alone. Take for example the circulation function. We did not know where to base our decision to set higher or lower targets for each library. Some of the challenging questions we needed to resolve were the following: Do we need to increase the target every year? If we do, would we have the required resources to meet such a target? The thought process was that we had to "map the behavior of the process" first to see the anticipated variations in circulation from month to month. Taking guidance from Donald J. Wheeler's book *Understanding Variation: The Key to Man-*

aging Chaos, we were able to map out "the voice of the process" (see Figure 13.11). The book provided a simple mathematical formula to determine the higher and lower limits of a process, along with the average score (variance analysis). We recorded monthly circulation numbers for a total of 12 months for a pilot library. This time period was selected simply because a year represents a full fiscal year and is usually the standard operating cycle.

After doing the analysis, we were able to determine what constituted an over-stretched target. If the library's upper limit were 21,200, we would be setting that library up for failure if we set the target at 25,000. What the 21,200 meant was that, at this time, this is the optimum target for this specific library during the summer months, given its current space and available resources. If nothing changed in that library's operating system (i.e., bigger building, more staff, or larger collection), we could not expect any change in the numbers. If our goal is to have 25,000 circulated items (based on a benchmark), our priority would be to concentrate on the capacity issues that prevent the library from attaining the next highest target and not the increase in circulation itself.

Variance analysis also tells the managers when to intervene and when to leave the process alone. If the upper and lower limits are 21,200 and 7,300, any fluctuation between those numbers is due to a "common cause" inherent in the system, whereas anything above the upper limit or below the lower limit is due to a "special cause." A manager should intervene only in special cause situations, unless the process needs to be improved or changed.

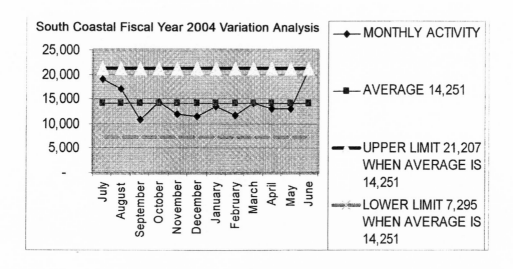

Figure 13.11 Example of Variation Analysis: Voice of Process.

Variance analysis also illustrates the "seasonality" of a library. As you can see, there is much higher circulation during the summer months and normal or lower circulation in the fall, winter, and spring. Obviously, this was a library close to the beach with a rise in summer population. In this example, because the summer months were distinctly "pushing" the higher limits up, we came to the conclusion that June, July and August had to be separated into a different chart because their numbers distorted the high, low, and average levels of the regular operating cycle. By separating these months, a manager will know what constitutes a special or common cause both in the normal season and in the high season (i.e., a manager cannot be expecting 21,000 circulated items in December). Therefore, this library's Balanced Scorecard would have to have two distinct targets for circulation: one for the high and one for the low seasons. It is at this point (i.e., once we've understood where we stand internally), that we would compare this library to its peers and determine the degree to which it needs to improve or not, and how far it has to go to meet a benchmarked performance.

Deployment

The final "D" phase involves everyone in an organization. It focuses on the following steps:
- Develop a communication plan
- Cascade the BSC throughout the organization
- Implement a systematic collection and analysis of data, evaluation and revision

DEVELOP A COMMUNICATION PLAN

Minds are like parachutes. They only function when they are open.
— Sir James Dewar,
Scientist (1877–1925)

Throughout the BSC development and deployment steps the most prominent word is "communication." Communication is like the air we breathe. It is vital to everything we do, including embarking on a new management system. People would want to know, every step of the way, what do you want me to do? What's in it for me? How will this change affect me? What will you do to help me make the change? How am I doing?

In developing a communication plan, the "W5" approach by Paul R. Niven discussed in the classic publication the *Balanced Scorecard: Step-by-Step: Maximizing Performance and Maintaining Results* seemed to capture the essence of our message. The five Ws stand for what, why, who, when, and where.

What and Why (*Purpose and message*): The organization must communicate to all levels of the organization what the Balanced Scorecard is, how it relates to other change initiatives, and how the scorecard fits with the overall strategy. Among many key messages, the communication plan might include training schedules, development and deployment timelines, status of implementation, and sustainability issues.

Who (Audience): The organization must determine who will be part of the implementation team. Different audiences will need to be targeted pre- and post-implementation depending on the size of the scorecard project. Plan to include the senior management team, steering committees or council groups, all employees and project leaders.

When (Frequency): During the development stage, communication among all participants is critical and is more frequent than the post-development stage. One of the success factors to developing and sustaining a scorecard is to keep communication lines open as an effective way of capturing the sense of urgency and enthusiasm generated at the start of the process.

Where and How (Delivery): Common methods of communicating during the pre- and post-implementation stages include e-mail, face-to-face meetings, workshops, video presentations, PowerPoint presentations, town hall meetings, news bulletins, and the use of a communication portal. Also, for each of the target audiences, a facilitator must be selected; this person will have the responsibility of leading discussions and sharing key information.

Table 13.4 below represents a simplified communication plan for your BSC project.

Table 13.4 Simplified Communication Plan			
Audience	*Purpose*	*Frequency & Method*	*Communicate*
Senior Leadership	-Gain commitment -Remove obstacles -Report progress -Prevent surprises	-Weekly -Direct contact	Exective Sponsor
Elected Officials	-Gain commitment -Remove obstacles -Report progress	-Annually -Direct contact	Executive Sponsor
Management	-Convey purpose -Explain concepts -Report progress -Gain commitment	-Weekly -E-mail -Management meetings -Intranet -Articles	Champion/Team Members

Who	What and Why	When	Where and How
Employees	-Convey purpose	-Monthly	Project Team
	-Introduce concepts	-E-mail	Members
	-Eliminate misconceptions	-Newsletters	
	-Report progress	-Intranet	
		-Town hall meetings	
Project Team	-Track progress	-Weekly	Champion
	-Assign tasks	-Team meetings	
	-Review expectations	-Status memos	
		-Intranet	

Source: Adapted from Paul R. Niven, Balanced Scorecard Step-by-Step: Maximizing Performance and Maintaining Results (2002).

CASCADE THE BSC THROUGHOUT THE ORGANIZATION

There is no greater teacher than responsibility.
— Warren Bennis,
Managing People Is
Like Herding Cats

A recent study by consulting firm Watson Wyatt revealed that only about half (49 percent) of employees understand the steps their companies are taking to reach their business goals. This represents a 20 percent decrease since 2000. This problem can be alleviated by cascading the scorecard to all levels of the organization.

Cascading is the process of developing and implementing aligned scorecards throughout the entire department — all the way down to the different divisions, sections, units, teams and individual employees of the organization. Each level of the organization develops strategic objectives and performance measures based on the scorecard of the group they report (Figure 13.12).

You would think that by having created a top level or overall scorecard, you have solved the problem of unclear goals and objectives. Not just yet. Employees need to know what roles they play in achieving the mission, vision, and strategic goals of the organization. As international consultant Watson Wyatt (2002) noted, "There is a tremendous positive impact to the bottom line when employees see strong connections between company goals and their jobs. Many employees aren't

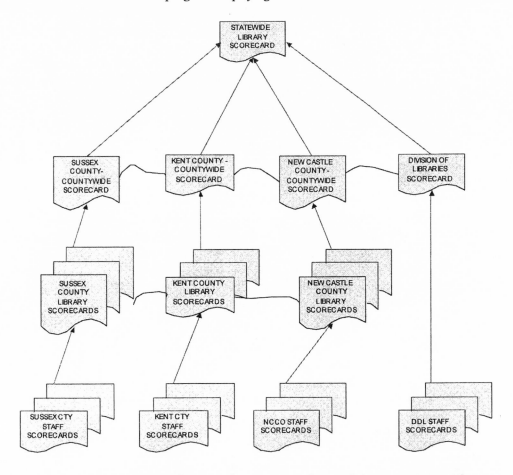

Figure 13.12 *Delaware Libraries' Map of Cascaded Scorecards.*

seeing that connection" [Work USA® 2002-Weathering the Storm: A Study of Employee Attitudes and Opinions].

Think about this for a moment: Do your frontline employees (reference staff, receptionists, and secretaries) know how their everyday duties contribute to the strategic plan? How about the managers and the ones above them? We all agree that it's nice to know about the overall measures of your organization. This knowledge gives you a solid sense that you and your leaders are headed in the right direction. However, does your frontline staff know what individual measures they are accountable for? How would they know what to monitor in their day-to-day operations?

In other words, it is *alignment* and *prioritization* time once more. It is at this stage that cascading scorecards are developed, down to each and every level of the organization as a way of aligning and defining how everyone can and will contribute toward the overall scorecard.

An important factor that needs to be considered is that a scorecard should be taken as a descriptive guide and not a prescriptive one. The key here is to cascade *leadership* and *ownership* of measures to employees, and not control decision making and creativity of employees. Ownership and leadership are the two ingredients that can lead to cultural change and sustainability.

At this step, some organizations may fool themselves by believing that frontline employees are incapable of analyzing and monitoring their own statistics. Therefore they do not need their own scorecards, although they are allowed to view the progression of the corporate scorecard. This could not be further from the truth. All employees want to do a good job. A majority are experts in their field, and they are the best ones to figure out how to do their jobs better. With the appropriate training, information, and resources needed to gain a solid understanding of the high-level organizational objectives and their strategic significance, the employees should be able to understand the organization's challenges and figure out how their jobs fit into this entire scheme. The questions that each employee might ask are: What can I measure and monitor at my level right now and in the future that would help the organization achieve its goals? Which overall strategic objectives can I *influence* based on what I am doing today? How can I do what I am doing today more effectively and efficiently?

Through the cascaded scorecards, the organization gains an abundance of rich and powerful performance data that provide new insights on how to improve performance. The data are invaluable, although their usefulness is compromised when not developed, monitored, and managed correctly. Automation can alleviate this problem. You can see some of the complexity that a cascaded scorecard can create in Figure 13.13.

> *Systematize the collection of data — analyze, evaluate and revise*
> *I haven't failed; I've found 10,000 ways that don't work.*
> — Thomas Edison
> (1847–1931)

The development of a Balanced Scorecard is not a one-time project. It is a continuous cycle of development, implementation, monitoring, and improvement. It follows the basic Deming quality principle of Plan-Do-Study-Act (PDSA) shown in Figure 13.14.

Opposite top: Figure 13.13 *Complexity of Administering the BSC Manually. Source: Screenshot from Balanced Scorecard software presentation of Insightformation, Bill Barberg, president.* **Bottom: Figure 13.4** *PDSA Cycle for High Quality Library Development.*

Cascading Cause & Effect

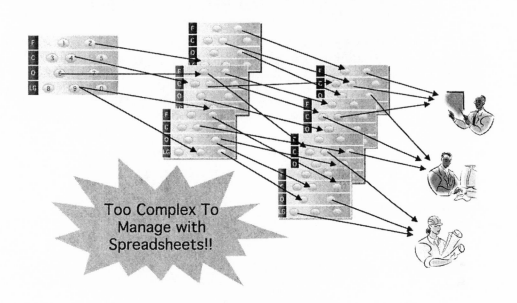

Too Complex To
Manage with
Spreadsheets!!

Vision, Mission, and Purpose	

PLAN
Develop and review
key requirements   to
carry out strategy

ACT
Standardize
processes that are
meeting key
requirements and
recommend
improvemen t
processes if needed

**High Quality
Library
Development**

DO
New processes are
designed and
implemented based
on results of
planning process

STUDY
Review and analyze
key performance
indicators

197

This continuous self-assessment process is actually what defines perfection. It is the continuous sharpening of the sword (knowledge, information, measures, and targets) to make sure we are keeping up with the current market trends and the continuous change in customer requirements. Playing strategically for the "checkmate" position is the name of the game.

It is a sure bet that at this moment you are thinking, "This is hard work" or "How would we ever have the expertise or time to do this?" It may sure seem this way at the beginning, because of inexperience in this new approach. Once you experience and master the Balanced Scorecard, it is going to become second nature to you. This is not to say that it will not take time to monitor it or update it, but maintenance will be a breeze compared to development. It will basically run itself, if set up properly and if ultimately automated. It will make a world of a difference.

Steady and sustained leadership is needed to make this successful. Senior leaders must provide employees with the needed resources, whether training or technology. They have to ensure that two-way communication lines are open. On the other side of the coin, all employees must know what they are accountable for by completing training and by getting actively engaged in the process. When accountabilities and roles are clear, both senior leaders and employees are equipped to use this innovative system as a powerful tool that supports and validates data-based decision making.

14

Maintaining and Improving Your Commitment to the Balanced Scorecard

"Individual commitment to a group effort— that is what makes a team work, a company work, a society work, a civilization work."
— Vince Lombardi

"It's about management and change first; measurement and technology are second."

— Howard Rohm,
Balanced Scorecard
Institute

The most important phrase here is *commitment* for change; first by leadership and then by the rest of the organization. It is important to remember that the Baldrige and BSC processes are not one-time projects. To keep the momentum going both systems need continuous monitoring and improvement, although sustaining the project generally gets easier with time.

The suggestions for how to sustain your Balanced Scorecard efforts are adapted from Howard Rohm and Larry Halbach of the Balanced Scorecard Institute. These guidelines were published online, in "A Balancing Act: Sustaining New Directions" in *Perform Magazine: Performance Management in Action*.

- *It's time for a change— avoid "business as usual."*

    Habits are hard to change. Until everyone gets used to managing within the scorecard framework, they will tend to fall back into their old ways of doing things. Just follow the system and change will come naturally with time. This is a great new opportunity to reorganize meetings based on strategic themes, initiatives, perspectives, or maybe all three. Meetings must remain focused not only on operational objectives but also goals for the future, and be *macro*-managing in nature instead of *micro*-managing.

- *Assign permanent Balanced Scorecard roles*

    The scorecard by its very nature assigns "owners" to measures. This simply means that a designated staff member becomes the responsible party for monitoring and achieving of that measure. A measure owner may not necessarily be the person collecting the data for the measure. The assignment of permanent BSC roles goes beyond that. It means staff or teams headed by a key manager can be assigned as owners of whole perspectives or themes. Regular meetings among those teams will ensure attention to and alignment between the strategic themes throughout the year and the years ahead.

- *Use the scorecard process to develop the strategic plan*

    Remember Table 10.2 in Chapter 10: old vs. new ways of strategic planning? The old way is useless and expensive if you give the assignment to a few administrative planners who end up hiring a consultant to do the plan anyway. In addition, the old way of updating the strategic plan was quite painful because of the lack of performance measures and targets that guide strategy implementation.

    Instead, practice revising and fine tuning your BSC as the new way of updating your strategic plan until it's a habit. Because the BSC allows for regular application and monitoring throughout the year, each strategy could continuously be reviewed by systematically revisiting the cause and effect linkages among objectives to ensure they make sense and are still valid.

- *Use the Balanced Scorecard strategic plan to drive budgeting and cost control*

    The BSC drives performance-based budgeting and activity-based costing (ABC), because the costs are activity- and program-driven instead of just fund-driven.

    As was noted before, each objective on the BSC is linked with an appropriate measure, target and owner, and also an initiative and a projected cost. Therefore, you can see that as the BSC is developed, you are basically allocating your budget by program or by initiative, and corresponding activities. Continuing to budget in this manner will focus and refine the use of available funds every time the BSC is reviewed and updated.

- *Continue to work on the strategic enablers: communication, change management practices, incentives, reporting results and prioritization initiatives*

    Change management does not happen for "one season," just as change does not happen overnight. Change management practices must be sustained before, during and after the development of the BSC. What does change management mean?

- It is sustaining the transparent, two-way communication channels throughout the whole organization. Leaders must continuously answer the "why" question so that employees need not guess what their leaders' visions and future plans are.
- It involves continuing to link scorecard measures and targets to staff performance plans, not as a way of micromanaging employees but as a way of keeping the momentum of the project. It also provides clarity for employees as to exactly what their roles and responsibilities are in the achievement of the overall strategy, from fiscal year to fiscal year.
- Change management makes reporting performance results and comparing actual versus expected results routine and almost reflexive activities. This will help with keeping track of progress. When differences arise, they will be questioned, which might lead to adjustment and refinement of targets.
- The most common pitfalls to sustainability, according to Charles Bloomfield and Bill Barberg of Insightformation, Inc., as discussed in the article "Bringing the Balanced Scorecard to Life: The Microsoft Balanced Scorecard Framework" (January 2004), are the following:

- *Measures do not focus on strategy*

  There must be alignment and cause and effect linkage between the measures and the strategy. An organization may have world-class benchmarks, but may be way off target with its strategy. In the words of one of the BSC founders, David P. Norton: "The biggest mistake that organizations make is thinking that the scorecard is just about measures. Quite often they will develop a list of financial and non-financial measures and believe they have a scorecard. This, I believe, is dangerous."

- *The BSC is not adequately explained*

  To be effective, a scorecard must be clearly communicated. The rest is self-explanatory.

- *Measures are tied into compensation or non-compensatory recognition too soon*

  A "fresh" balanced scorecard is not the final one. It will almost always need to be fine tuned and refined. Objectives and measures will be changed and improved over time because the initial measures may be incorrect, inaccurate, or incomplete. If recognition is tied into the scorecard too soon, you might be endorsing premature rewards and recognition for actions and results that need further refinements.

- *There is no accountability*

    Each and every person in an organization should drive change. Therefore, everyone's performance must be linked to some objective, measure or target. Everyone should be an "owner" of something.

- *Employees not empowered*

    In order for employees to own change and be motivated to perform, they must be provided with all the necessary resources to enable them to do their jobs. Employees need training and information to make decisions; clear lines of authority and responsibility to forge ahead; and the leader's trust to remain motivated and engaged.

- *There are too many initiatives*

    In the case of large organizations there may be many initiatives that cross interdepartmentally. This can lead to duplication of efforts that waste resources and time. One way to avoid this problem is to do a cross matching of scorecard objectives and identify where the crossing initiatives occur. The department where the initiative makes the biggest impact should be the one that is assigned that initiative. At times, organizations may simply have too many initiatives to begin with. This can lead to unfocused strategies and resources, which can spread the organization too thin. In this case, a reevaluation and reprioritization of initiatives must take place each fiscal year.

Conclusion

"You cannot acquire experience by making experiments. You cannot create experience. You must undergo it."
— Albert Camus
(1913–1960)

We firmly believe that the powerful system presented in this book will bring "mission effectiveness" to your organization. Despite the fact that it may be impossible to exactly measure your organization's current and future impact on the community, we guarantee that your collective decision making, organizational efficiency, effectiveness and productivity will be greatly enhanced.

By using the Baldrige Criteria and the Balanced Scorecard as a single system, you will raise visibility of the things that really matter: your competent and motivated employees, systematic and effective processes, and your leaders making confident decisions based on data, and ultimately the delight of your customers. What is your *proven* value to the citizens and communities you serve, libraries? Better measure that, because it will be improving and rising exponentially.

We hope that by sharing our quality journey we have shed some light on your organization's quest for excellence. Most of all, we hope that your perspective on performance excellence has, at the very least, evolved to the next level. At DDL, we are continuing to make incremental progress. We have started a cycle of continuous improvement, and it really does get better with every turn. Remember at the beginning of the book we urged you to "follow the yellow brick road?" Well, we did, and we are about to see the wizard....

References

Arveson, Paul. (1999). "Translating Performance Metrics from the Private to the Public Sector." Retrieved November 23, 2005. http://www.balancedscorecard.org/

———. (2004). "The Revolution in Strategic Planning." Retrieved November 8, 2005. http://www.balancedscorecard.org/

Band, William A. (1991). *Creating Value for Customers*. New York: John Wiley & Sons.

Bankoski, Linda, A. and Carmen Traxler. (n.d.). *Roots and Wings: Six Sigma and the Baldrige Criteria*. Concurrent Session B6 presented at the 30th Annual Delaware Quality Conference, Dover, Delaware.

Barberg, Bill. (2005). "Balanced Scorecard Best Practices: Understanding Leading Measures." Retrieved May 12, 2006. http://www.insightformation.com/

———, and Charles Bloomfield. (January 2004). "Bringing the Balanced Scorecard to Life: The Microsoft Balanced Scorecard Framework." Retrieved May 30, 2006. http://www.insightformation.com/

Batten, Joe. (1993). *Building a Total Quality Culture*. Milwaukee: ASQ Quality Press.

Bertot, John C., Charles R. McClure, and Paul T. Yeager. (May 2005). *Public Libraries and the Internet 2004: Survey Results and Findings*. Funded by the Bill and Melinda Gates Foundation and the American Library Association.

Bhote, Keki R. (2002). *The Ultimate Six Sigma: Beyond Quality Excellence to Total Business Excellence*. New York: Amacom.

Blanchard, Ken, John Carlos, and Alan Randolph. (2001). *The Three Keys to Empowerment. San Francisco: Berrett-Koehler Publishers.

Block, Peter. (1987). *The Empowered Manager: Positive Political Skills at Work*. San Francisco: Jossey-Bass.

Blazey, Mark L. (2005). *Baldrige in Brief*. Milwaukee: ASQ Quality Press.

———. (2006). *Insights to Performance Excellence 2006*. Milwaukee: ASQ Quality Press.

Brown, Mark Graham. (2006). *Baldrige Award Winning Quality 2006*. New York: Productivity Press.

———. (1996). *Keeping Score: Using the Right Metrics to Drive World-Class Performance*. New York: Productivity Press.

Buckingham, Marcus, and Curt Coffman. (1999). *First, Break All the Rules*. Princeton, N.J.: The Gallup Organization.

Carter, Louis, David Giber, and Marshall Goldsmith. (2001). *Best Practices in Organizational Development and Change*. San Francisco: Jossey-Bass/Pfeiffer.

Craig, John, and Smith D. Douglas. (April 2003). *Strategic Planning and Performance-Based Budgeting: In the District of Columbia*. PowerPoint presentation at the annual Performance Measurement for Government Conference, Washington D.C.

Champy, James. (1995). *Reengineering Management*. New York: HarperCollins.

Cohen, Marshal. (2006). *Why Customers Do What They Do*. New York: McGraw Hill.

D'Aprix, Roger. (1996). *Communicating for Change*. San Francisco: Jossey-Bass.

Dohm, Arlene. (July 2000). "Gauging the

Labor Force Effects of Retiring Baby Boomers." *Monthly Labor Review.*

Eckes, George. (2001). *The Six Sigma Revolution: How General Electric and Others Turned Process into Profits.* New York: John Wiley & Sons.

Goal/QPC, Continuous Improvement and Standardization. (n.d.) *The Total Quality Management Circle.* Retrieved April 14, 2003. http://www.goalqpc.com.

Institute of Museum and Library Services. (1999). *Outcomes-Based Evaluation for IMLS-Funded Projects for Libraries and Museums.* Retrieved January 27, 2003. http://www.imls.gov/grants/current/crnt_obebasics.htm.

Hamel, Gary, and C.K. Prahalad. (1994). *Competing for the Future.* Boston: Harvard Business School.

Hammer, Mike, and James Champy. (1993). *Reengineering the Corporation.* New York: HarperCollins.

Hunt, V. Daniel. (1993). *Quality Management for Government: A Guide for Federal, State and Local Implementation.* Milwaukee: ASQC Quality Press.

Kaplan, Robert, and David Norton. (1996). *The Balanced Scorecard: Translating Strategy into Action.* Boston: Harvard Business School Press.

_____, and David Norton. (2001). *The Strategy-Focused Organization.* Boston: Harvard Business School Press.

Keehley, Patricia, Steven Medlin, Sue MacBride, and Laura Longmire. (1997). *Benchmarking for Best Practices in the Public Sector.* San Francisco: Jossey-Bass.

Kiser, Kenneth J., and Sashkin Marshall. (1993). *Putting Total Quality Management to Work.* San Francisco: Berrett-Koehler Publishers.

Lawson, Robin L. (1993). *Creating a Customer-Centered Culture: Leadership in Quality, Innovation, and Speed.* Milwaukee: ASQC Quality Press.

Lawler, E., S.A. Mohrman, and G. Benson. (2001). *Organizing for High Performance.* San Francisco: Jossey-Bass.

Miller, George L., and LaRue L. Krumm.

(1992). *The Whats, Whys, and Hows of Quality.* Milwaukee: ASQC Quality Press.

National Institute of Standards and Technology. (2006). *Criteria for Performance Excellence* [Brochure]. National Institute of Standards and Technology. Gaithersburg, MD.

National Institute of Standards and Technology. (2003). *Criteria for Performance Excellence.* Retrieved from http://www.quality.nist.gov.

National Institute of Standards and Technology. (2002). "Baldrige National Quality Program." In *Baldrige, Six Sigma, and ISO: Understanding Your Options.* Retrieved from http://www.quality.nist.gov.

National Standards of Science and Technology Fact Sheet 2005. (2005). Retrieved from http://www.quality.nist.gov.

Nelson, Sandra. (2001). *The New Planning for Results: A Streamlined Approach.* Washington, D.C.: Government Printing Office.

Niven, Paul. (2003). *Balanced Scorecard Step-By-Step: Government and Non-Profit Agencies.* New York: John Wiley and Sons.

_____. (2002). *Balanced Scorecard Step-By-Step: Maximizing Performance and Maintaining Results.* New York: John Wiley and Sons.

Noe, Raymond A. (1998). *Employee Training and Development.* New York: Irwin/McGraw-Hill.

Norton, D. P. "Aligning Strategy and Performance with the Balanced Scorecard." Interview conducted by Eric P. Marquardt. Retrieved March 30, 2001. http://www.cfshq,com/task/NTC/balanced.htm.

Osborne, D., and T. Gaebler. (1992). *Reinventing Government.* Reading, Mass.: Addison-Wesley.

O'Neill, Mary Beth. (2000). *Executive Coaching with Backbone and Heart.* San Francisco: Jossey-Bass.

Pande, Peter S., Robert P. Neuman, and Roland R. Cavanagh. (2000). *The Six Sigma Way: How GE, Motorola, and Other Top Companies Are Honing Their Performance.* New York: McGraw-Hill.

Procurement Executive's Association (July 8, 1999). *Guide to a Balanced Scorecard Perfor-*

mance Management Methodology [Online]. http://oamweb.osec.doc.gov/bsc/guide.htm.

Rao, Ashok, et al. (2000). *Total Quality Management: A Cross-Functional Perspective.* New York: John Wiley and Sons.

Rogers, Everett. (1962). *Diffusion of Innovations.* New York: Free Press of Glencoe.

Rohm, Howard. (n.d.). "A Balancing Act." *Perform* Volume 2, Issue 2. Retrieved March 22, 2006. http://www.balancedscorecard. org/.

_____, and Larry Halbach. (n.d.). "A *Balancing Act: Sustaining New Directions*" *Perform* Volume 3, Issue 2. Retrieved March 22, 2006. http://www.balancedscorecard.org/

_____, (2000). "Improve Public Sector Results with a Balanced Scorecard: Nine Steps to Success." Retrieved May 12, 2006 http://www.balancedscorecard.org/.

Rushkoff, David. (2005). *Get Back in the Box: Innovation from the Inside Out.* New York: Collins.

Scholtes, Peter. (1998). *The Leader's Handbook.* New York: McGraw-Hill.

Silverman, Lori L., and Annabeth L. Propst. (1999). *Critical Shift: The Future of Quality in Organizational Performance.* Milwaukee: ASQC Quality Press.

Sirota, David, Brian Usilaner, and Michelle Weber. "Sustaining Quality Improvement." *The Total Quality Review,* March–April 1994: 23–30.

Smith, Howard, and Peter Fingar. (2003). *Business Process Management: The Third Wave.* Milwaukee: ASQC Quality Press.

Smith, Ralph. (June 7, 2004). "Building the

Balanced Scorecard in Public Sector Organizations." *Orion Development Group.* Retrieved May 31, 2006. http://www.odgroup. com/articles.

Timm, Paul R. (2001). *Customer Service: Career Success Through Customer Satisfaction.* Upper Saddle River, N.J.: Prentice-Hall.

Treacy, Michael, and Frederick D. Wiersema. (1995). *The Discipline of Market Leaders.* Reading, Massachusetts: Addison-Wesley.

Watson Wyatt Worldwide Research Reports. "Work USA® 2002-Weathering the Storm: A Study of Employee Attitudes and Opinions." Available online at http://watsonwyatt.com/research/resrender.asp?id=w-557 &page=1.

Wheeler, Donald J. (2000). *Understanding Variation: The Key to Managing Chaos.* Knoxville: SPC Press.

Weidner, Marv. (April 2003). *How to Lead Organizational and Cultural Change to Achieve Results for Customers.* PowerPoint presentation at the annual Performance Measurement for Government conference, Washington, D.C.

Xerox. (1988). *Competitive Benchmarking: The Path to a Leadership Position.* Stamford: Xerox Corp.

Zook, Chris, and James Allen. (2001). *Profit from the Core: Growth Strategy in an Era of Turbulence.* Boston: Bain & Company, Inc., and Harvard Business School Press.

_____. (2004). *Beyond the Core: Expand Your Market Without Abandoning Your Roots.* Boston: Bain & Company, Inc., and Harvard Business School Press.

Index

Index